The Adventure Express Game

Jim Bennett

"All Aboard!"

This booklet is dedicated to all teachers
who strive to provide
an exciting and memorable educational experience
for their students.

ISBN: 978-1-4357-5052-4

The Game

The Adventure Express game is a fun way to incorporate cooperative learning activities and projects into a math/science curriculum. The game also has a classroom management component which helps the teacher keep students on task.

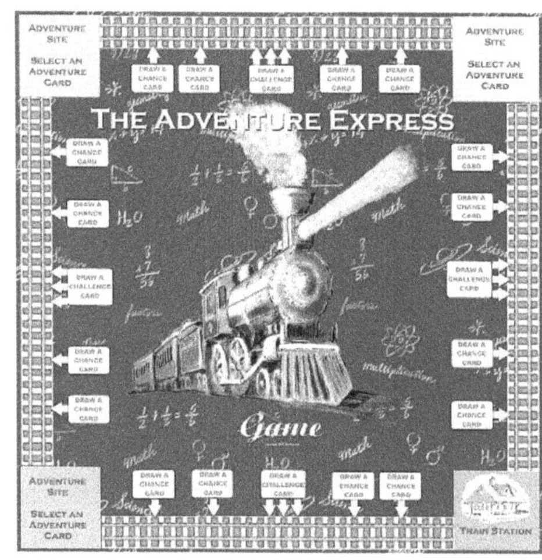

The Adventure Express, used alongside an existing math/science curriculum, adds a sense of adventure, excitement, and fun. The premise is the students are riding a train which takes them to different adventure sites. Each adventure is a project which is either selected by the teacher or drawn at random from a set of cards. The game is designed for grades 5 – 7.

Each class that plays the game works as a team—or in this case, the students pretend to be passengers who travel together on a train. They do not move around the board individually—they must move as a team. If more than one class is playing the game, an element of competition can be introduced to see which train can move around the board faster and accumulate the most points.

How the Game Is Played

The object of the game is to move around the board as quickly as possible, successfully complete adventure projects, and earn game points. Students earn game points by doing the challenges, completing the projects, doing well on tests and by passing the train station – like passing "Go" in Monopoly.

The trains start at the train station and move clockwise around the game board. When they reach a corner square, either the teacher will give them a project assignment or they will draw a project card which instructs them to build or create something or conduct a hands-on experiment. Thirty sample projects are included in this manual. All these activities can be customized to meet the needs of any upper elementary math or science curriculum.

If a train lands on any of the Challenge or Chance spaces, a student draws the appropriate card and the class follows the instructions on the cards. Chance cards are similar to chance cards in other games. Challenge cards involve math/science problems which usually have a cooperative learning component and include a time limit.

The speed at which a class moves around the board is determined by spinning a spinner or rolling a number cube. This is based on classroom behavior – if students use their class time wisely, they get to move faster than they would if they waste time in class.

How to Use Adventure Time

ADVENTURE TIME

TODAY	TOTAL
+3:00	17:30

Adventure Time adds an effective classroom management component to the game. Adventure Time is an adaptation of Dr. Fred Jones' "Preferred Activity Time" strategy. Visit *www.fredjones.com* for additional information on Dr. Jones' recommendations for using PAT.

I keep a record on the board of "Adventure Time" which is based on how diligently the class works and does not waste time. The more diligently the students work, the more adventure time they can earn. Wasting time results in a loss of time (minus instead of plus).

How Adventure Time Works

- The class "earns" time by working—not goofing off. This is accomplished when everyone is prepared for class and works diligently during class.
- The class "loses" time when anyone is unprepared, is not working, is daydreaming, talking, or in other ways "using up the time" unproductively.
- The teacher keeps score for the day and adds up the total.
- If the students gain a minimum number of minutes in a day (I use 3 minutes), they get to spin the spinner and advance the number of spaces spun. If they gain a higher number of minutes (I use 5 minutes), they get to double whatever number they spin. If they earn an even higher number minutes (I use 8), they get to triple whatever they spin.
- When the class reaches a corner square, the students get to spend their accumulated time working on a project in class. When they reach the train station, they get to play games such as math baseball.
- The requirements for spinning are set by the teacher. Ideally, the class should be able to reach a corner square in more than a week and no more than two to three weeks.

Adventure Time is based on the premise that students are motivated to work toward a goal which is fun for them. Students usually understand the concept of working to save up time so they can do something they enjoy. It is clear to them that when they waste time, they are using up the time and cannot have it later.

The goal is to motivate students to work diligently and not waste time during class. In practice, the teacher simply keeps a daily record of the time the students "save" and gives it back to them all in one lump sum when they land on a corner square. For example, if the class saves an average of 3 minutes a day and it takes them 12 days to reach a corner square, they will have a total of 36 minutes to spend during class working on projects. Projects that are not completed in class, would have to be finished at home.

If the class falls below the minimum daily time requirement set by the teacher (for example, I set a minimum of 3 minutes), they do not get to spin that day. If they earn at least the minimum, they get to spin the spinner which will tell them to advance 1, 2, or 3 spaces.

The teacher's goal is to encourage students to earn more than the minimum number of minutes. To do this, I set two additional levels above the minimum time requirement. If their daily time is equal to or above the next level (5 minutes), they get to double whatever number they spin on the spinner. If they reach a third level (8 minutes), they triple what they spin.

Note: if a class is particularly immature and has difficulty working with delayed rewards, they will need to "cash in" their time faster than a more mature class. My sixth grade students are mature enough to handle waiting two to three weeks to "cash in" their time.

The Adventure Time behavior management system is simple, easy, and effective. Basically, whenever a behavior problem arises in one of my classes, all I have to do is calmly stroll over to the Adventure Time scoreboard and begin to subtract time. Immediately, students will correct themselves and get back on task. I rarely even have to say a word. If someone happens to say, "He's taking away our time!," I respond with "No, I'm not taking away your time. You just used up the time. I'm simply keeping score for you. You can use it now or save it for later."

The Projects

There are 30 project cards and corresponding fact sheets provided in this manual. The teacher may modify these or create other projects as needed.

How to Score the Game

If there are two or more trains, the classes can have a competition for game points. I give game points for projects using the following scale: A = 4 points; B = 3 points; C = 2 points; D = 1 point. I also give game points for test scores using the same scale.

How the Game Is Won

The game is designed so it can be played as long as you like. The winning team (train) is the one that has earned the most points when the game ends. When I created the game, my classes played it for the entire school year.

Setting Up the Game

A game board is needed. A full-color poster is available from the Math Squad store at www.*Cafepress.com/mathsquad*. This poster includes the game board and pictures of 3 trains that can be separated from the game board section. Clothespins can be used as game pieces.

You may create your own game board using the poster that is reproduced in black and white on one of the following pages or on the back cover in full color. Simply photocopy a transparency and project it onto a piece of large paper. Sharpie pens work great for drawing the game board. A third option is to cut out and tape together the 12 sections at the end of this booklet.

In the introduction to the game, students are instructed to draw pictures of themselves which are cut out and pasted onto the passenger cars so they create a collage of all the students in their class aboard the train. The teacher can make a picture of himself/herself and paste it in the locomotive window. The train can also be colored with markers and given a name.

If you want to distribute train tickets, a page of tickets is included for photocopying. On the first day of school I dress up as the conductor and distribute and punch the tickets when I introduce the game. An inexpensive costume conductor's hat can be purchased at many costume shops or online at *www.lynchs.com*.

Small tokens (colored clothes pins which can be clipped to the edge of the poster work great) are used to indicate each team's position on the game board. The trains start at the train station and move clock-wise around the board. The number of spaces (railroad ties) that a team moves each day is determined either by spinning a spinner or rolling a number cube.

Adventure Bucks

Students can earn Adventure bucks (blackline master included) for doing well on warm-up quizzes and homework, chance cards, or as special rewards for working a challenging problem. Often, when I see that the class is looking bored or tired, I will "perk things up" by offering an adventure buck for the first student who can solve a particular problem.

They can use their Adventure Bucks to buy homework and quiz passes (master included), answer checks (at the teacher's discretion), permission to sit in a particular desk, play chess, or other privileges.

Students are "fined" if they talk out of turn or do not have materials. I "rent" pencils when students don't have pencils. My pencils are "the worst pencils in the world" - small, golf pencils with no erasers.

Additional Items

I have additional items available at the Cafepress.com Math Squad store. These include a large "All Aboard" poster, a full-color spinner design, conductor's hat emblem, and pins for awards.

There are also numerous items on the pages in the rest of this booklet.

Key to the Materials in the Rest of this Booklet

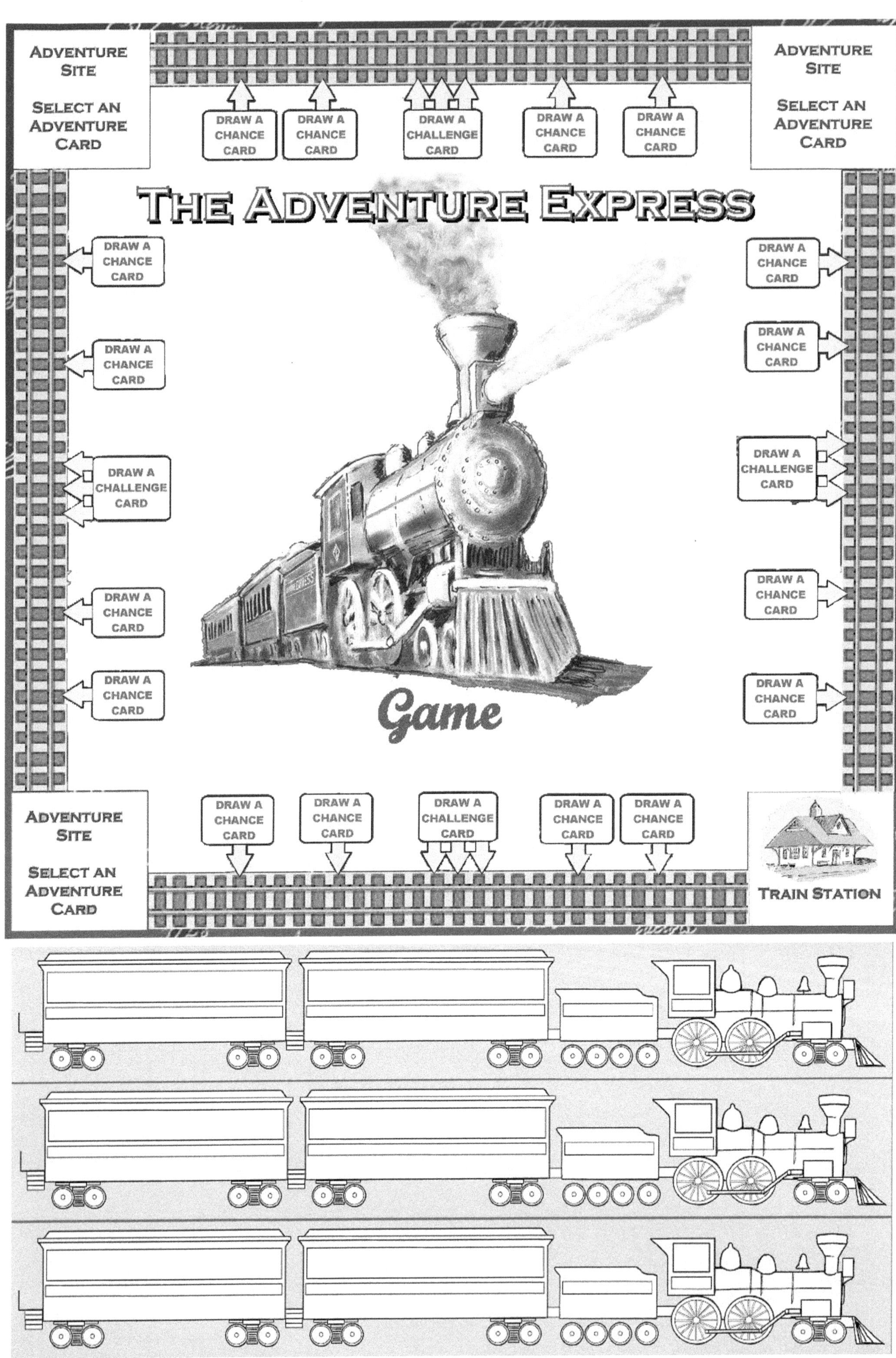

Adventure Site
Select an Adventure Card
Draw a Chance Card
Draw a Chance Card
Draw a Challenge Card
Draw a Chance Card
Draw a Chance Card
Adventure Site
Select an Adventure Card
The Adventure Express
Draw a Chance Card
Draw a Chance Card
Draw a Challenge Card
Draw a Chance Card
Draw a Chance Card
Draw a Chance Card
Draw a Chance Card
Draw a Challenge Card
Draw a Chance Card
Draw a Chance Card
Game
Adventure Site
Select an Adventure Card
Draw a Chance Card
Draw a Chance Card
Draw a Challenge Card
Draw a Chance Card
Draw a Chance Card
Train Station

The Adventure Express
ONE ROUNDTRIP

The Adventure Express
ONE ROUNDTRIP

The Adventure Express
ONE ROUNDTRIP

The Adventure Express
ONE ROUNDTRIP

The Adventure Express
ONE ROUNDTRIP

The Adventure Express
ONE ROUNDTRIP

The Adventure Express
ONE ROUNDTRIP

The Adventure Express
ONE ROUNDTRIP

The Adventure Express
ONE ROUNDTRIP

The Adventure Express
ONE ROUNDTRIP

The Adventure Express
ONE ROUNDTRIP

The Adventure Express
ONE ROUNDTRIP

1
ADVENTURE BUCK
1
STRIVE FOR EXCELLENCE
NEVER NEVER GIVE UP!
DESIRE + ACTIONS + CONSISTENCY = SUCCESS

1
ADVENTURE BUCK
1
STRIVE FOR EXCELLENCE
NEVER NEVER GIVE UP!
DESIRE + ACTIONS + CONSISTENCY = SUCCESS

1
ADVENTURE BUCK
1
STRIVE FOR EXCELLENCE
NEVER NEVER GIVE UP!
DESIRE + ACTIONS + CONSISTENCY = SUCCESS

1
ADVENTURE BUCK
1
STRIVE FOR EXCELLENCE
NEVER NEVER GIVE UP!
DESIRE + ACTIONS + CONSISTENCY = SUCCESS

1
ADVENTURE BUCK
1
STRIVE FOR EXCELLENCE
NEVER NEVER GIVE UP!
DESIRE + ACTIONS + CONSISTENCY = SUCCESS

1
ADVENTURE BUCK
1
STRIVE FOR EXCELLENCE
NEVER NEVER GIVE UP!
DESIRE + ACTIONS + CONSISTENCY = SUCCESS

1
ADVENTURE BUCK
1
STRIVE FOR EXCELLENCE
NEVER NEVER GIVE UP!
DESIRE + ACTIONS + CONSISTENCY = SUCCESS

1
ADVENTURE BUCK
1
STRIVE FOR EXCELLENCE
NEVER NEVER GIVE UP!
DESIRE + ACTIONS + CONSISTENCY = SUCCESS

1
ADVENTURE BUCK
1
STRIVE FOR EXCELLENCE
NEVER NEVER GIVE UP!
DESIRE + ACTIONS + CONSISTENCY = SUCCESS

1
ADVENTURE BUCK
1
STRIVE FOR EXCELLENCE
NEVER NEVER GIVE UP!
DESIRE + ACTIONS + CONSISTENCY = SUCCESS

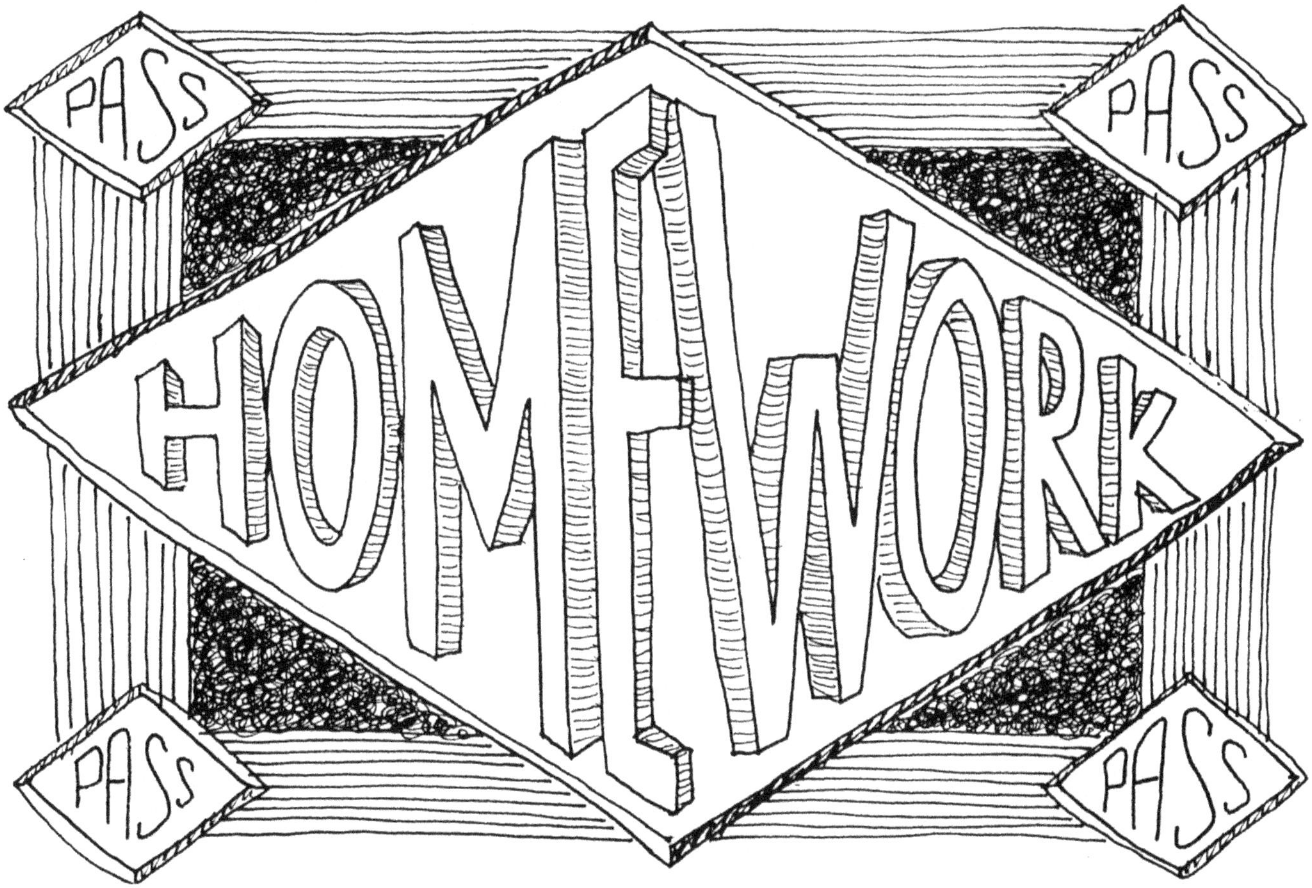
PASS
PASS
HOMEWORK
PASS
PASS

OFFICIAL
QUIZ
PASS

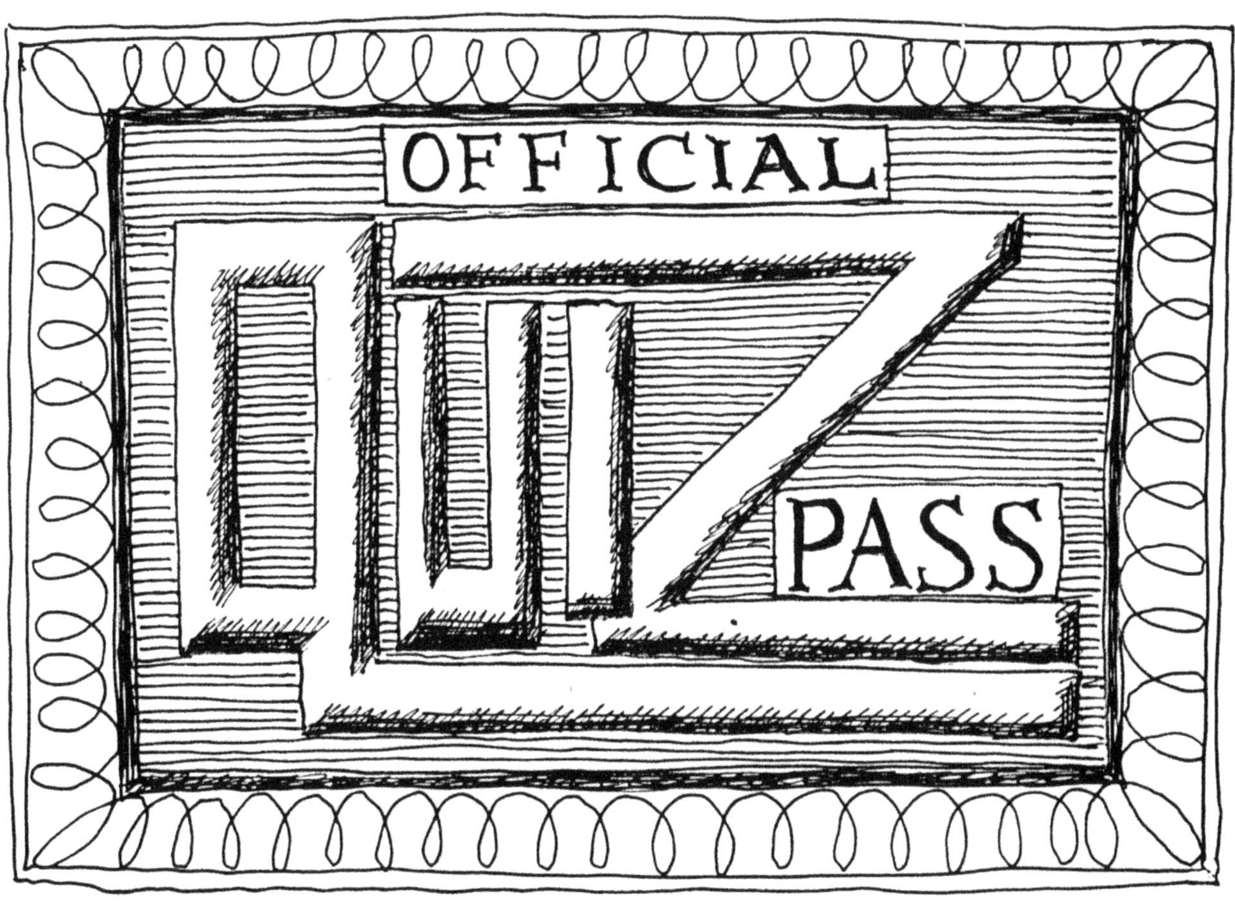

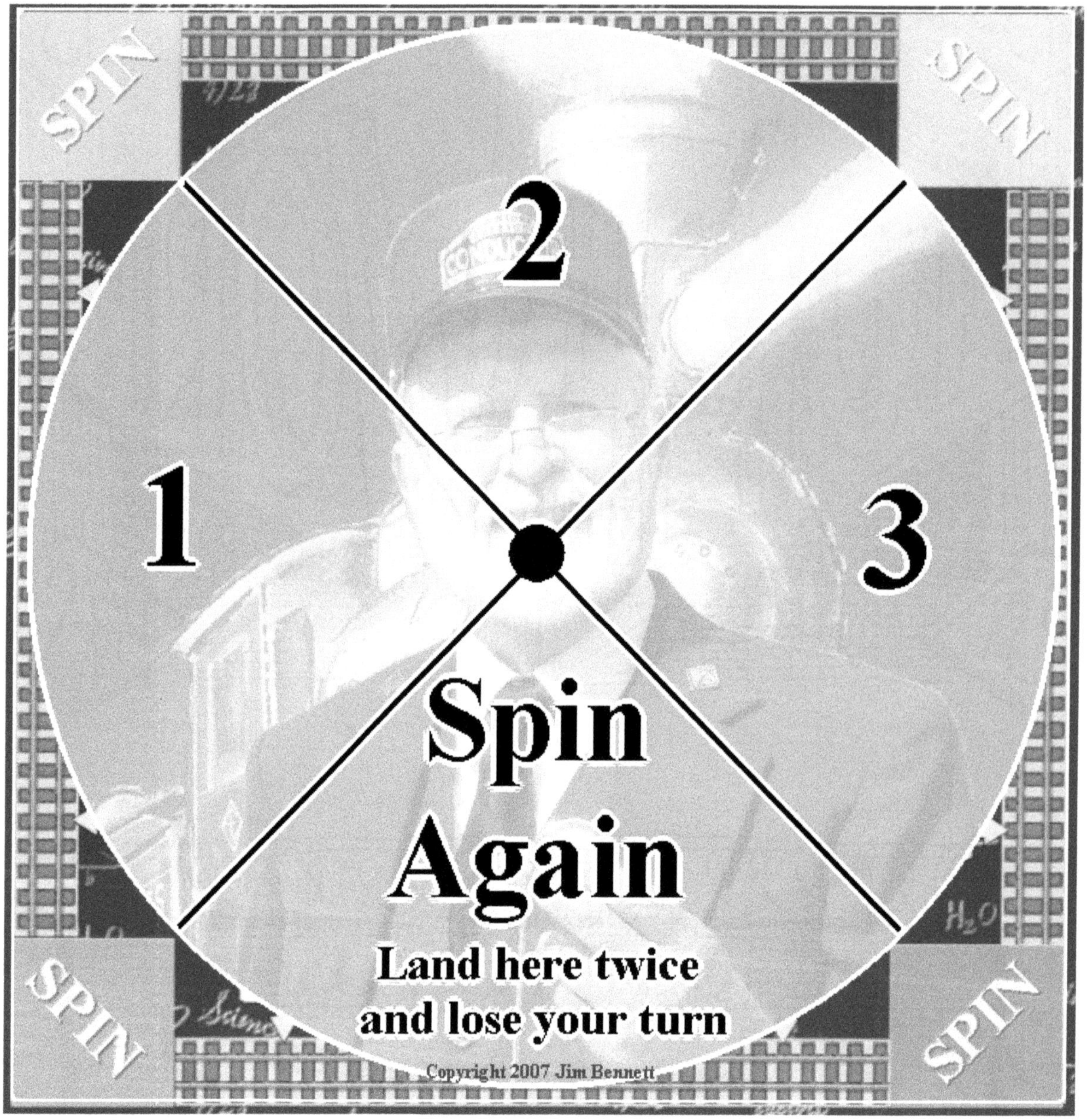
SPIN
SPIN
SPIN
SPIN
1
2
3
Spin Again
Land here twice and lose your turn
Copyright 2007 Jim Bennett

Color the trains, cut them out, and attach to clothespins for game pieces.

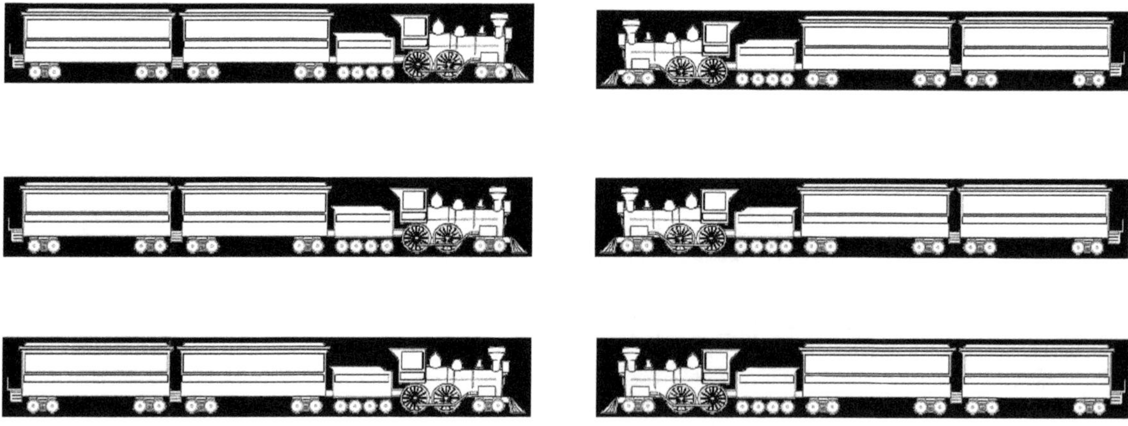

THE

ADVENTURE EXPRESS

TRAVELER'S PROJECT BOOK

Name ______________________________

"All Aboard!"

Train Schedule

All Aboard for
THE ADVENTURE EXPRESS!

This ___*(year)*___ we are going to be doing some exciting and fun things in ___*(Name of subjects)*___.

Our class will be playing a game called "The Adventure Express" where we'll pretend to take a train ride. The game is full of surprises and ___*(challenges)*___.

The train conductor is ___*(teacher's name)*___.

The Adventure Express game begins at the ___*(train)*___ ___*(station)*___. The object of the game is to go around the track as many times as you can, complete the adventures, and accumulate ___*(time)*___ and ___*(points)*___. Since you travel with your class, you'll need to help each other. You and your classmates are on the same ___*(train)*___.

Each day your class can earn "Adventure Time." When the whole class ___*(completes)*___ work on time, ___*(follows)*___ all the rules, and doesn't ___*(waste)*___ time, the class will be rewarded with special "Adventure Time."

If you earn ___*(three)*___ or more minutes for the day, you'll get to ___*(spin)*___ a spinner. The more time you earn, the farther you'll get to ___*(move)*___. If you earn less than three minutes, you don't get to ___*(spin)*___.

The time you earn each day will be saved up so you

can use it to do a ___(project)___ in class.

The ___(Rules)___ of the Game

The rules of the game are ___(simple)___. Do these things to win.

1. Always strive to do your very best, Your teacher and your ___(parents)___ expect you to do your best. Doing your best means that you must be prompt and fully ___(prepared)___ when class begins. That means having pencils, papers and books at your ___(desk)___.
2. Respect and encourage one another. Encourage others to do their ___(best)___. Teasing and name-calling when a person makes a mistake are simply not allowed.
3. When you arrive in this room, take your ___(seat)___ and begin to work on the activity written on the board. Don't wait for the ___(teacher)___ to tell you to get started.
4. When I hold up my hand and say "OK class, let me have your eyes up here," you are supposed to hold up your hand immediately, ___(stop)___ whatever you are doing and look at me. Keep your hand raised until I lower ___(mine)___.
5. When the class lines up and moves to another location, you are expected to be ___(quiet)___, orderly, and not waste ___(time)___.
6. Obey all ___(school)___ rules (dress code , conduct, punctuality, etc.).

Do these things and you'll save up ___(time)___ to work on fun projects in class. Every day that you get a 5 (perfect score) on a quiz and also homework, you will earn an "Adventure Buck." Adventure Bucks may also be given out during class as ___(special)___ rewards for good work. Adventure Bucks can be used to buy a number of things like homework ___(passes)___ and quiz ___(passes)___ and ___(treats)___.

Be careful though. If you forget to bring a ___(pencil)___ or your ___(book)___ to class, you will have to rent them by paying the ___(conductor)___ with Adventure Bucks.

ADVENTURE BUCK

STRIVE FOR EXCELLENCE

NEVER NEVER GIVE UP!

DESIRE + ACTIONS + CONSISTENCY = SUCCESS

You will need the following supplies for this class: ___(supply list)___

____

____

____

Getting started

Your first homework assignment is to ___(cover)___ your textbooks and make certain you have all your supplies. If you cover your book with paper and decorate it, you can earn an additional Adventure Buck.

Today, you must get ready to board the train. Draw a small picture of your ___(head)___ and shoulders in the little rectangle on the right. Then cut it out and we'll paste it into the window of the ___(train)___. If you have time, your class can also ___(color)___ your train.

All aboard!

Chance	Chance	Chance
The train is making great time. Advance one space.	The train is making great time. Advance one space.	The train is making great time. Advance one space.
Chance The train is making excellent time. Advance two spaces.	**Chance** The train is making excellent time. Advance 2 spaces.	**Chance** If everyone in class has a textbook, advance 2 spaces.
Chance If everyone in class has a textbook, advance 2 spaces. If not, go back one space.	**Chance** If everyone in class has a textbook, advance 2 spaces. If not, go back one space.	**Chance** If everyone in class has a pen or pencil, advance 1 space. If not, go back one space.
Chance If everyone in class did his or her homework, advance 2 spaces. If not, go back 2 spaces.	**Chance** If everyone in class did his or her homework, advance 2 spaces. If not, go back 2 spaces	**Chance** The conductor's treat: an extra Adventure Buck for everyone today!
Chance The conductor's treat: move ahead one space.	**Chance** The conductor's treat: take another spin on the spinner!.	**Chance** The conductor's treat: take another spin on the spinner!.
Chance A tree fell across the tracks and must be removed. Go back one space.	**Chance** A cow is on the tracks. The train is delayed. Go back one space.	**Chance** The train needs to stop for water in the boiler. Go back one space.
Chance The train is delayed while work is being done on the tracks. Go back one space.	**Chance** The train is delayed while work is being done on the tracks. Go back one space.	**Chance** Anyone who does not have his or her textbook must pay one Adventure Buck.
Chance Anyone who does not have a pen or pencil must pay one Adventure Buck.	**Chance** Oops! The train breaks down and must stop for repairs. Go back 2 spaces.	**Chance** Oops! The train breaks down and must stop for repairs. Go back 2 spaces.

CHALLENGE	**CHALLENGE**
Form groups of 3-5 students. Add together all the digits of everyone's phone numbers (7 digits) in each group. Average them. Show all the work. Time limit: 5 minutes Reward: move ahead 2 spaces	Form groups of 3-5 students. Within each group, count the number of letters in each person's full name. Average them. Show all the work. Time limit: 5 minutes Reward: move ahead 3 spaces
CHALLENGE Students work with partners. Time how long each of you can hold your breath. What is the difference between the two times? Time limit: 5 minutes Reward: move ahead 1 space	**CHALLENGE** Students work with partners. Take each person's pulse. Make a bar graph. Time limit: 4 minutes Reward: move ahead 1 space
CHALLENGE Form groups of 3-5 students. Each person measure in centimeters <u>and</u> inches the distance between the tips of the thumb and little finger when the hand is stretched as far as possible. Record the results and calculate the averages. Round to the nearest whole numbers. Time limit: 6 minutes Reward: move ahead 3 spaces	**CHALLENGE** Form groups of 3-5 students. Each person measure the length and width of his or her right shoe. Write the measurement as a whole or mixed number to the nearest eighth of an inch. Then divide the width into the length and write the answer as a mixed number. Show all work. Time limit: 5 minutes Reward: move ahead 3 spaces
CHALLENGE Form groups of 3-5 students. Without using any kind of measuring, each person tries to draw a square that measures about 4 inches on a side. After everyone has drawn a square, measure them to see which is longer—the width or the height. Can you conclude that there a tendency for people to draw a square either too wide or too tall? Time limit: 4 minutes Reward: move ahead 1 space	**CHALLENGE** Form groups of 3-5 students. Each person in the group writes out a portion of the multiplication tables (2's through 9's) so that the group completes all the multiplication facts. Check over your answers. Time limit: 4 minutes Reward: move ahead 2 spaces

Challenge	Challenge
Form groups of 3-5 students. Assign a number to all the letters of the alphabet (A = 1, B = 2, C = 3, etc.) Using this system, each person in the group converts the letters in his or her first name to numbers. Then find the sum of the numbers. Next, each person does the same for his or her last name. Finally, divide the last name number by the first name number. Calculate to the nearest tenth. Time limit: 5 minutes Reward: move ahead 3 spaces	Form groups of 3-5 students. Assign a number to each month of the year (Jan. = 1, Feb = 2, etc.). Each person in the group makes a fraction by putting his or her birth month in the numerator and 12 in the denominator. Add all the fractions in the group together and write the answer in simplist form. Time limit: 5 minutes Reward: move ahead 3 spaces
Challenge Form groups of 3-5 students. Each person in the group flips a coin 10 times. Record the results using tally marks. Total everyone's results and make a circle graph for the group that shows the percent that was heads and the percent that was tails. Time limit: 5 minutes Reward: move ahead 2 spaces	**Challenge** Work with partners. Time each person to see how long he or she can stand and hold his or her math book straight in front of themselves without bending the arms. Make a bar graph. Time limit: 5 minutes Reward: move ahead 1 space
Challenge Form groups of 3-5 students. Each person sees how many words he or she can make using just the letters from his or her first and last names. Each group writes down the total number of words that were created and the total number of letters in all the names. Write these as a ratio. Time limit: 6 minutes Reward: move ahead 2 spaces	**Challenge** Form groups of 3-5 students. Record the pulse (beats per minute) of each person in the group. Make a stem and leaf plot. Time limit: 6 minutes Reward: move ahead 1 space
Challenge Form groups of 3-5 students. Each person in the group counts the letters in his or her last name and then divides that number by 2.5. Find the sum of all those quotients for the group. Show all work. Time limit: 5 minutes Reward: move ahead 3 spaces	**Challenge** Form groups of 3-5 students. Each person in the group writes down his or her zip code and then multiplies it by the length in inches of his or her arm. Measure from the tips of his or her fingers to the shoulder (round to the nearest inch). Time limit: 6 minutes Reward: move ahead 3 spaces

Challenge

Form groups of 3-5 students. Each person writes down what he or she thinks is the height in centimeters of an object in the room selected by the teacher. Find the average the group's guesses. Measure the actual height and calculate the difference between the guess and the measurement.

Time limit: 5 minutes

Reward: move ahead 2 spaces

Challenge

Form groups of 3-5 students. Each person writes his or full name normal size (the size he or she usually writes). Measure the length in millimeters. Add all the measurements together and convert the sum to centimeters. Find something in the room that is close to this length.

Time limit: 6 minutes

Reward: move ahead 3 spaces

Challenge

Form groups of 3-5 students. Everyone writes down his or her birthday. Pick one person in the group and calculate how many days remain until the person's next birthday.

Time limit: 5 minutes

Reward: move ahead 3 spaces

Challenge

Work with a partner. Calculate each of your ages in days. Don't forget that leap years have 366 days. For the years since you were born, if the year number is divisible by 4, it was a leap year.

Time limit: 6 minutes

Reward: move ahead 3 spaces

Challenge

Form groups of 3-5 students. Each person writes the number of doors in his or her house (or apartment). Pass papers leftward (or clockwise). The next person multiplies the first number by the number of windows in his or her house. Exchange papers. Each person now divides the previous answer by the number of rooms in his or her house. Write the answer as a whole or mixed number.

Time limit: 5 minutes
Reward: move ahead 2 spaces

Challenge

Work with a partner. Measure the distance that each of you walks when you take 5 normal steps in a straight line. Divide this distance by 5 to get the length of an average step. Pace the length of your classroom. Using this data, estimate the actual length of the room.

Time limit: 5 minutes

Reward: move ahead 2 spaces

Challenge

Form groups of 3-5 students. Without measuring, each person draws 3 straight lines of different lengths on a sheet of paper. Exchange papers, and then measure the 3 lines in centimeters. Create a stem and leaf plot from all the measurements in the whole group.

Time limit: 5 minutes
Reward: move ahead 3 spaces

Challenge

Work with a partner. Measure each other's height and also the distance each of you can reach when your arms are stretched out to the sides as far as possible. What is the difference between the two numbers? Can you draw any conclusions?

Time limit: 4 minutes

Reward: move ahead 2 spaces

Your adventure takes place in

AN AIRPLANE

Your adventure takes place in

A HOT AIR BALLOON

Your adventure takes place on

A CLIFF OVERLOOKING A CANYON

Your adventure takes place in

A CASTLE

Your adventure takes place in

A DARK CAVE

Your adventure takes place in

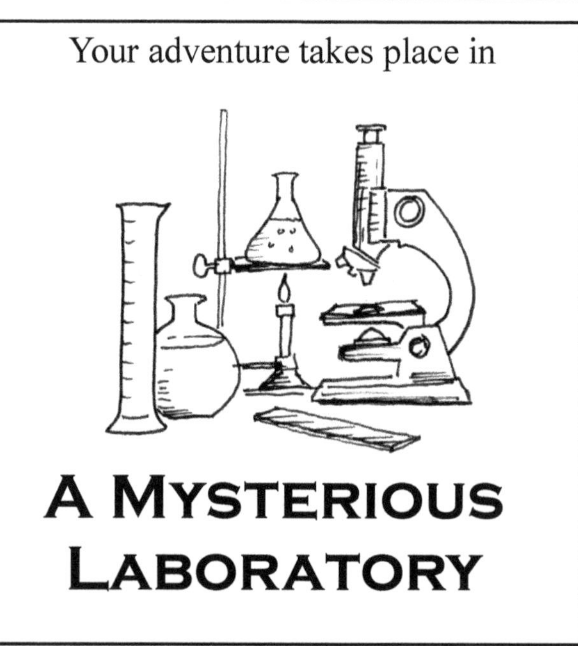

A MYSTERIOUS LABORATORY

Your adventure takes place in

AN OLD CHURCH

Your adventure takes place in

A HOT DESERT

Your adventure takes place in

THE LAND OF THE ESKIMOS

Your adventure takes place on

TREASURE ISLAND

Your adventure takes place in

A JUNGLE

Your adventure takes place in

AN ABANDONED MINE

Your adventure takes place on

A HIGH MOUNTAIN

Your adventure takes place in

A MUSIC CONSERVATORY

Your adventure takes place at

A NUMBER FACTORY

Your adventure takes place in

AN OBSERVATORY

Your adventure takes place in

A RACE CAR

Your adventure takes place in

A ROBOT WORKSHOP

Your adventure takes place in

A Rocket

Your adventure takes place in

A Speed Boat

Your adventure takes place in

A Time Machine

Your adventure takes place in

A Tall Tower

Your adventure takes place

Under the Sea

Your adventure takes place at

An Active Volcano

Your adventure takes place in

An Amusement Park

Your adventure takes place in

A Museum

Your adventure takes place in

A Sailing Ship

Your adventure involves

A Video Game

Your adventure takes place in

A Chef's Kitchen

Your adventure takes place on

The Internet

The Airplane Adventure

Name ______________________

Project: Build a paper airplane. Have a contest to see whose airplane goes the farthest distance and whose airplane stays in the air the longest amount of time.

Materials: a standard 8 1/2 X 11 sheet of paper, glue, scissors, tape. Paper clips and popsicle sticks are optional.

How to build it:
You want to build an airplane that flies the farthest as straight as possible. You may use only one sheet of paper. You may fold, cut, glue, or use tape in building your airplane. You may also use paper clips and popsicle sticks if you want to.

Research: There is a lot of information on the Internet about how to build really good paper airplanes. There are also books on the subject.

Data: Make three flights. For each flight, record the distance traveled and the time that your airplane was in the air.

Follow-up: Fill in the chart below showing the distances and times of the flights and also the average distance and time for the three flights. Below the chart show the average speed of your airplane (distance divided by time) and the average speed converted into miles or kilometers per hour.

Flight	Distance	Time
Flight 1		
Flight 2		
Flight 3		
Averages		

Average speed = ____________________ = ____________________

The Amusement Park Adventure Name ____________________

Project: Make a rollercoaster.

Materials: You may use any materials that you like including cardboard, aluminum foil, paper, tape, glue, etc. Use a marble to roll down the track.

If you use paper, you can make a track just like the one in the illustration.

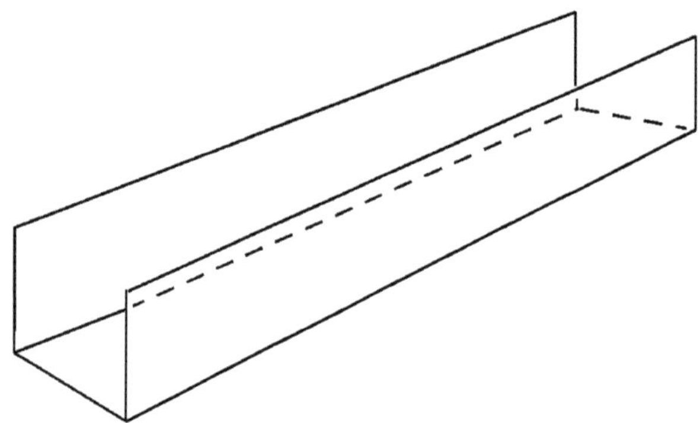

How to make it: You can put anything you like underneath to support the track including chairs, tables, boxes, and books. Try to design your rollercoaster so it has hills, turns, and loops. Loops are the most difficult. Use a stopwatch to measure the time it takes for the marble to travel from the beginning to the end.

Data: Place a photograph of your rollercoaster in the space below.

The old conductor says, "Tape the track together in sections. Begin with a long downhill section off of a chair or table so the marble will gain speed."

The Art Museum Adventure

Name ____________________

Project: Find an example of art that has to do with math or science.

How to do it: Use the Internet to find examples of art where the artists have used math or science. Print out an example and paste it in the box below. Show it to your class and explain what it is about the art that has to do with math or science.

What does the example have to do with math or science? ____________________

____

____

The Hot Air Balloon Adventure Name ________________________

Project: Build a hot air balloon and see how high you can make it go.

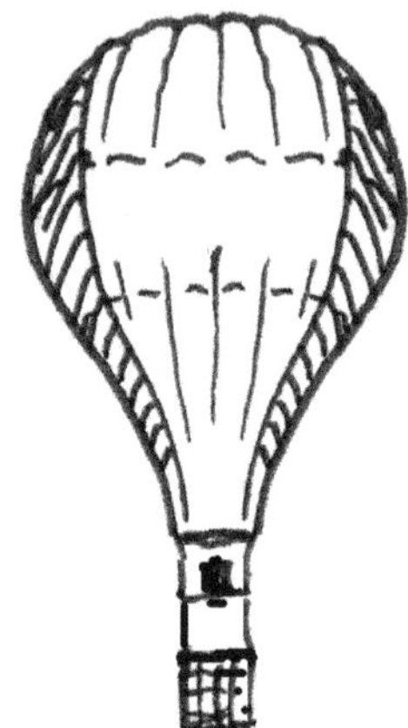

Materials: a light-weight plastic bag (such as a dry-cleaning or grocery bag) or tissue paper. A blow-dryer set to medium or better yet a hot air popcorn popper is used to fill the balloon with hot air.

How to build it
The material that you use for your balloon must be extremely light-weight. If you use tissue paper, you will have to glue "boat" shaped panels together (see illustration). These shapes should be about four times as long as the widest measurement. Eight of these shapes will make a balloon.

The "boat" shape

Carefully overlap the edges slightly and glue together into a balloon shape. You can do this over an inflated rubber balloon to hold the shape, and then pop the balloon after the glue has dried.

Safety: do not use a flame to heat the balloon.

Research: You can find information on the Internet about how to build different kinds of hot-air balloons.

Data: See how high you can make your balloon rise. Use a device such as the Estes AltiTrak or inclinometer to measure the height. Designs for inclinometers are on the Internet.

Follow-up: Record the maximum height that your balloon reaches.

My hot-air balloon rose to a height of ____________________

The old conductor says, "The larger you make your balloon, the more hot air it will hold and the higher it can go! Also, if the "mouth" of the balloon where the hot air goes in is smaller than the rest of the balloon, the hot air will stay in better."

The Cliff Overlooking a Canyon Adventure

Name ________________________

Project: Build 4 kinds of "bridges" to cross the canyon to the other side and test them to see which is the strongest.

Materials: Paper patterns for the bridges, glue, paper cup, tape, pennies.

How to build it: Build 4 bridges out of paper—triangular, rectangular, corrugated, and cylindrical. Don't use tape; only glue.

Note: The patterns for the bridges are on the next two pages.

Build a testing device—a "basket" made with a large paper cup and a strong loop of paper. You may use tape. Put pennies in the cup to see how many your bridge will support before it collapses.

Data: Test the bridges over a 4-inch space between desk tops. See how many pennies you can put in the cup before the bridge collapses. Record and graph the results. (Most bridges will hold about 100 pennies; some will hold about 300!)

Follow-up: What shape holds the most weight? Why?

____

____

Data	**Graph**

Use these for the Cliff Overlooking a Canyon Adventure

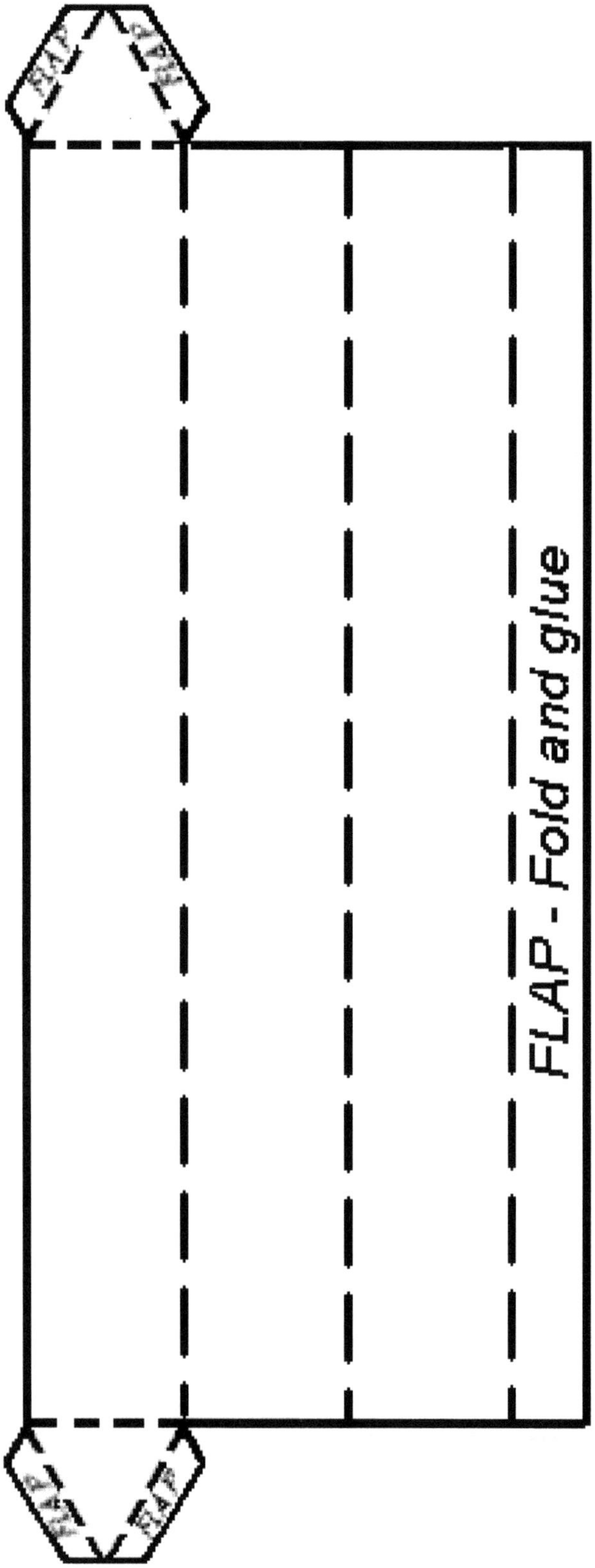

FLAP

FLAP

FLAP - Fold and glue

FLAP

FLAP

Triangular pattern

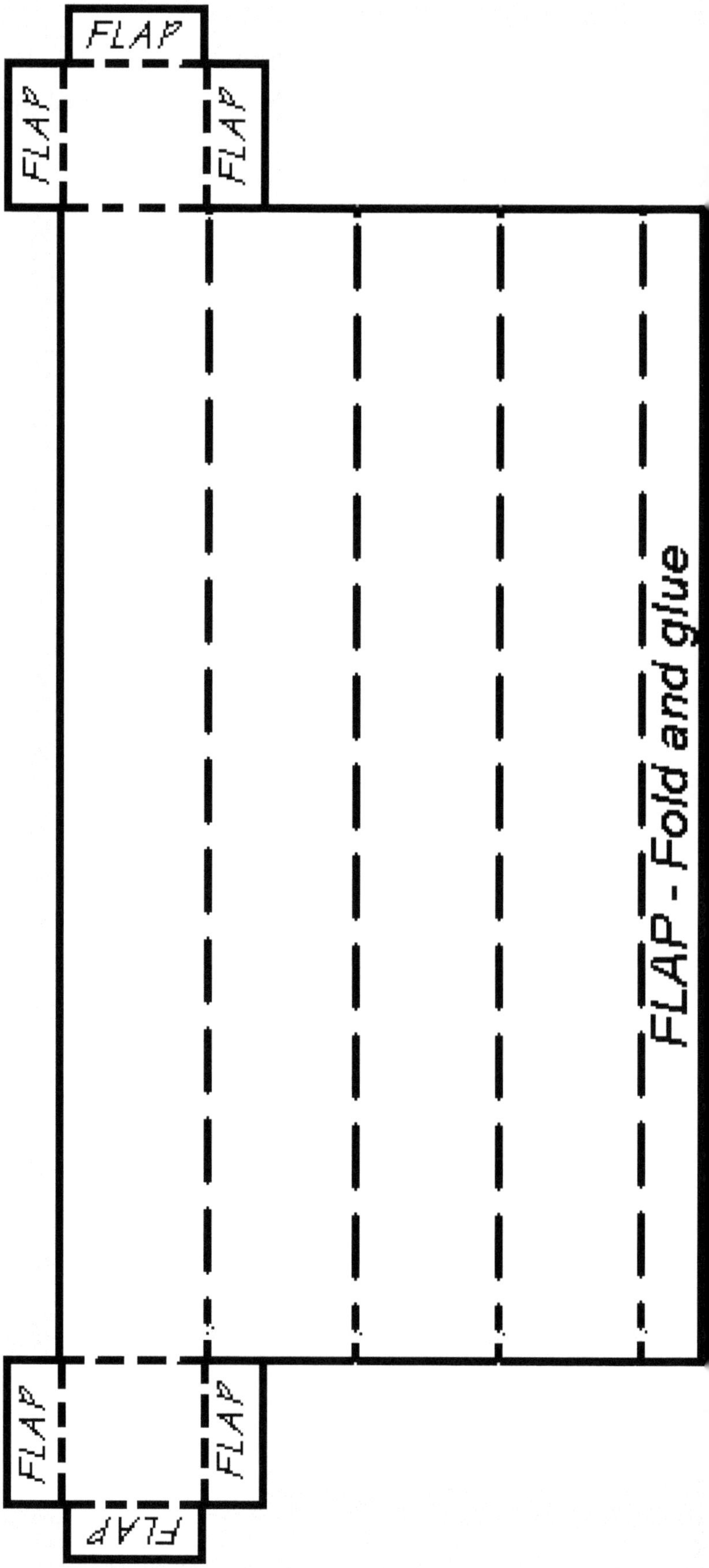

FLAP

FLAP

FLAP

FLAP - Fold and glue

FLAP

FLAP

FLAP

Rectangular pattern

Use this page for the Cliff Overlooking a Canyon Adventure

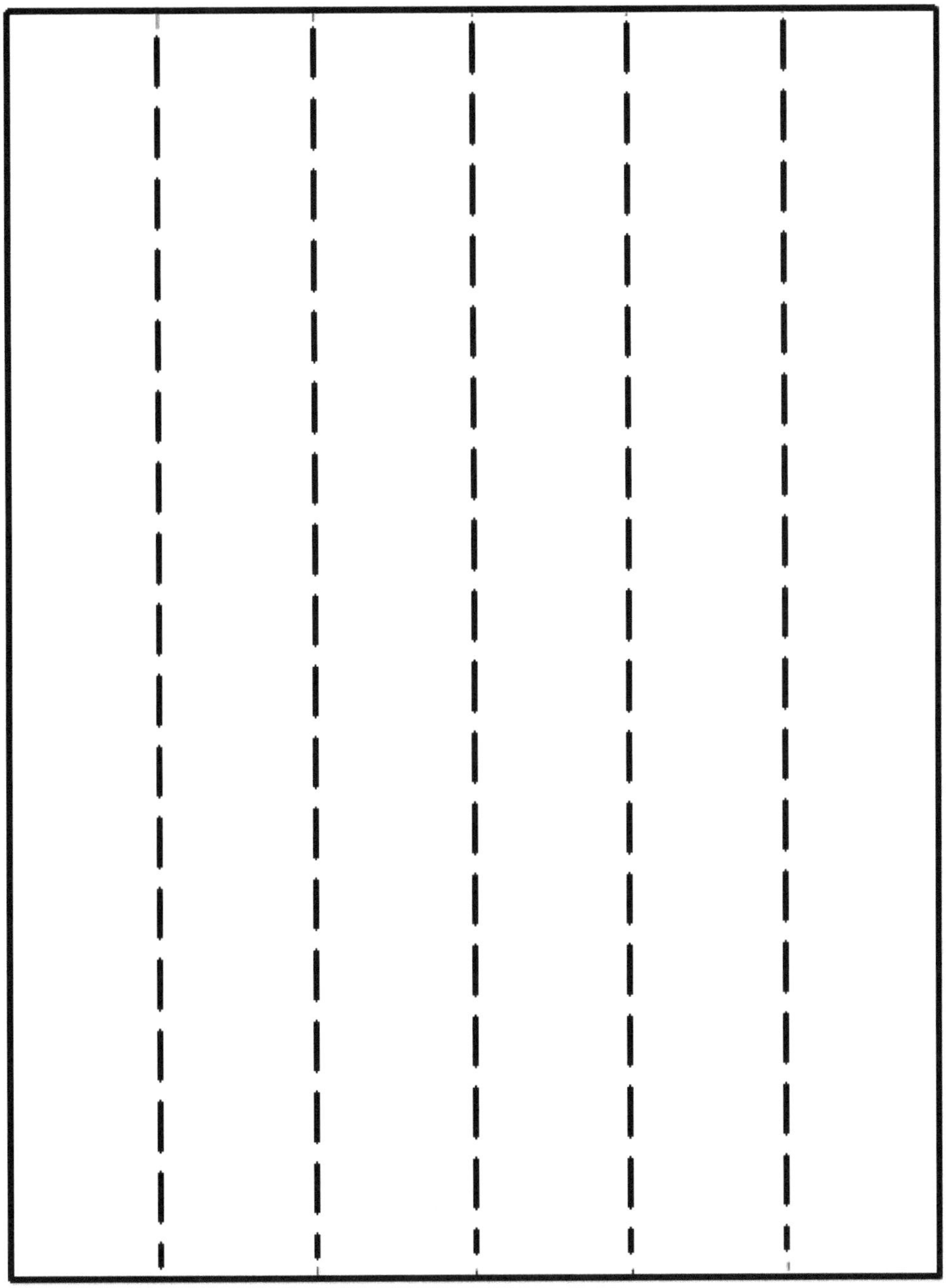

Make a "basket" for holding the pennies the bridges will support Use a large-size paper cup, a handle made from paper folded over several times, and tape.

The corrugated bridge: Make 5 folds (like a fan). Then glue the two sides together.

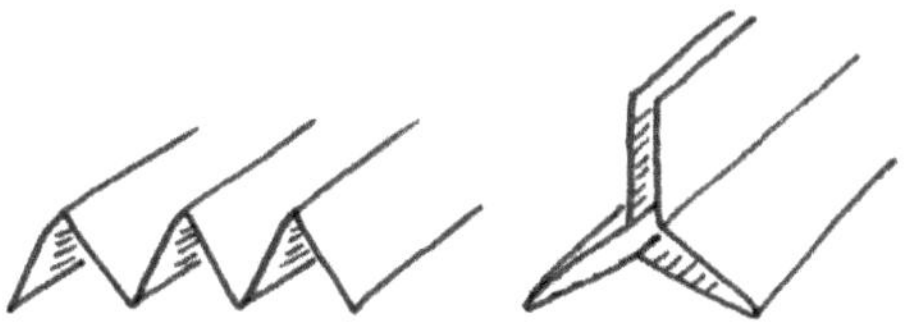

To make a cylinder, roll a piece of paper that is 4 sections of this pattern.

The Castle Adventure

Name ___________________________

Project: Make a scale model of a castle.

Materials: Use cardboard boxes and any other materials you want.

How to build it: Research castles on the Internet or at your library. Make certain that your model has all the most important parts of a real castle.

Make your model "to scale" by using the figure below as a gauge. The figure represents a man who is 6-feet tall

Data: Calculate the surface area of the external walls if your castle were actual size. Use square feet.

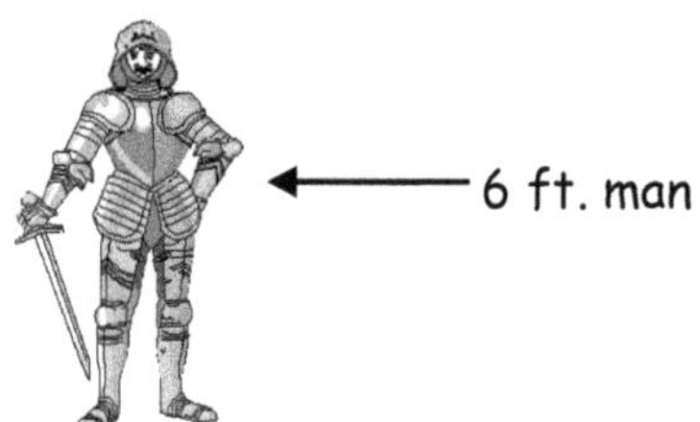

1. Calculate the areas of each of the rectangular shapes that make up the exterior walls. (The area of a rectangle equals the length multiplied by the width.)

2. Add them all together to get the total surface area.

The Cave Adventure

Name ______________________

Project: "Grow" stalactites and stalagmites.

Materials: 2 containers, 3-4 cups of water, Epsom salts (magnesium sulfate), a 24" piece of heavy cotton string or wool yarn, 2 metal washers for weights, 1 plate, a camera to photograph your results.

How to do it: Dissolve as much Epsom salts as you can into very warm water (120-140 °F) . Pour this solution into two containers. Set the plate between the containers, then put one end of the string in each container, and suspend the string between them. The string should be at least 3 inches above the plate. Let the string remain in place for several days. Do not touch or move it.

What happens: You will see that water soaks the entire string and drips off of the string at the low point between the containers. You will also see that deposits form where the water drips -- both from the string and onto the plate.

Data: After a few days, check to see if any material has built up on the string. An icicle-like formation should form downward on the string and upward on the plate. Photograph your results and attach the picture to this sheet.

Follow-up: How are real stalactites and stalagmites formed in a similar way?

____

____

____

____

____

____

____

The Internet Adventure Name ____________________

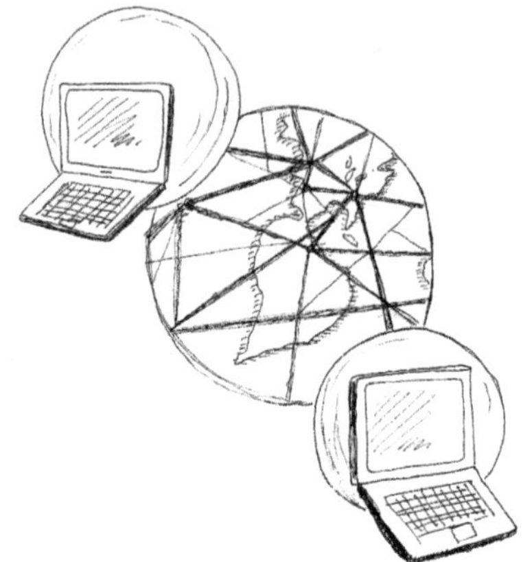

Project: Make a webpage.

How to do it: You can use one of the sites that provides free hosting. If you don't know HTML, make sure they provide an easy-to-use template for building a site.

Suggested Subjects: How to use an abacus, the history of algebra, atoms, Banneker, the Bible and math, binary code, Boole, calculators, careers that use math, casting out nines, chemical bonds, codes, computers, digital recording, Diophantus, $E=mc^2$, Einstein, exponents, Fibonacci, factors, fractals, geometry, golden ratio, googol. hypoteneuse, imaginary numbers, infinity, integers, intelligent design in creation, light and color, math jokes, matrix, mazes, Mendelbrot, molecules, music and math, Newton, numbers, Pascal, percentage, pi, polygons, puzzles, Pythagoras, robots, rockets, Rubik's cube, Sierpinski's triangle, space travel, square roots, tesseract, topology, triangles, tricks with numbers, weather and math, why we need to learn math, A Wrinkle In Time, zero.

My URL: ____________________________

The Title of My Site: ________________________

The Subject of My Site: ______________________________________

____

____

The Mysterious Laboratory Adventure Name ________________

Project: Make Silly Putty or Slime

Materials for Silly Putty: 2 c. white all-purpose glue, 1 c. liquid starch, food coloring (optional), Containers to mix & store

How to make it: Pour the glue into a container (big enough to use your hands for mixing). Add food coloring. Gradually add the starch to the glue using your hand to mix the 2 liquids. The mixing takes 10-15 minutes to reach the consistency of silly putty. It may seem like the mixture will not come together, but it will. Add more glue if the mixture seems too thick— more starch if too thin. Store the silly putty in airtight container.

Materials for Slime: Borax, white glue, food coloring (optional), Ziploc bags, measuring cups and spoons.

How to make it: Stir 1 Tbs. of borax into a cup of water. Stir until completely dissolved. Make 1/2 cup of 50% water—50% white glue solution. Pour equal parts of the borax solution to equal parts of the glue solution into a Ziploc bag. 1/2 cup of each will make a cup of slime. Add a couple drops of food coloring. Seal bag and knead the mixture. Dig in and have fun. Remember to wash your hands after playing.

Keep your Silly Putty or Slime in the sealed bag in the refrigerator when not playing with it to keep it longer. Unfortunately it may eventually dry out or grow mold. Just throw it out and start again!

These are not edible and are definitely not good for carpets or furniture. To keep almost indefinitely, leave in ziploc bag in refrigerator. Not a bad idea to wash hands before (so it doesn't grow mold) and after (so mom will let you eat dinner) playing with it.

Follow-up: Silly Putty and Slime are polymers. Name some of the physical characteristics of Silly Putty and Slime.

____

____

____

____

____

The Old Church Adventure

Name ______________________

Project: Create a "stained glass" window

Materials: a template, an 8 1/2 x 11" piece of treated acetate—the kind use as transparencies on overhead projectors, Marvy colored markers, black Puffy paint in applicator bottle, 9 x 12" black poster paper.

How to do it: Use one of the 4 templates supplied or make a drawing of your own. Lay the acetate over the template and fill in the shapes with color. When you are finished coloring all the shapes, turn the acetate over and trace all the edges of the shapes with the Puffy paint. Make a frame for your stained glass out of black poster paper. Hang your stained glass in front of a window.

Research: How do our eyes perceive colors? What is the color spectrum? Write your answers in the space below.

____

____

____

____

____

____

____

____

____

____

____

____

____

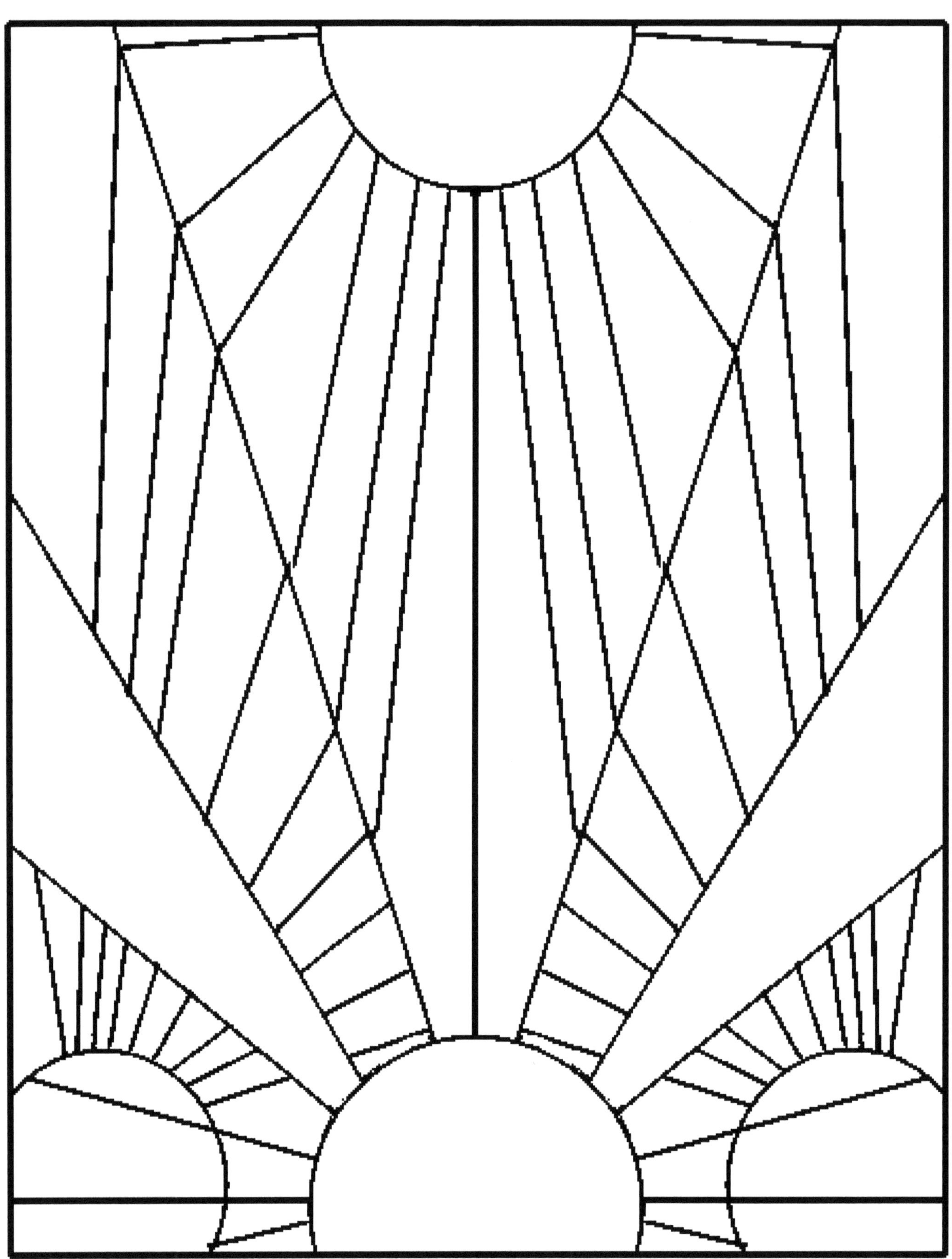

The Hot Desert Adventure

Name ____________________

Project: Make a thermometer.

MATERIALS: clear, plastic bottle (11oz. water bottle works), water, rubbing alcohol, clear plastic drinking straw, modeling clay, food coloring

How to make it: Fill about 1/4 of the bottle full with equal parts of water and rubbing alcohol. Add a few drops of food coloring. Put the straw in the bottle, so it touches the liquid but not the bottom. Use the modeling clay to seal the neck of the bottle, so the straw stays in place. (Make sure the straw does not touch the bottom of the bottle.)

Research: Place your "thermometer" in the refrigerator for a minute. Remove it and hold your hands around the bottom of the bottle. Observe what happens.

Data: What happened? Can you explain why it happened?

____

____

____

____

____

____

____

____

____

____

____

Treasure Island Adventure Name ___________________________

Project: Make a map of Math treasure Island.

Materials: Smooth watercolor paper, pencil, eraser, black <u>waterproof</u> pen, ruler, tea.

How to do it: Use the map below as a model.
Draw lightly with a pencil first. When your lines are correct, go over them with ink.

Use a legend of scale on the map to show how many inches equal how many miles. Make a border that has coordinates marked on it. Use math terms you have studied for all the names of the features on the map. If you have used waterproof ink, you can age the map by soaking it with coffee or tea. Let it dry flat. Make a list of all the features with their coordinates.

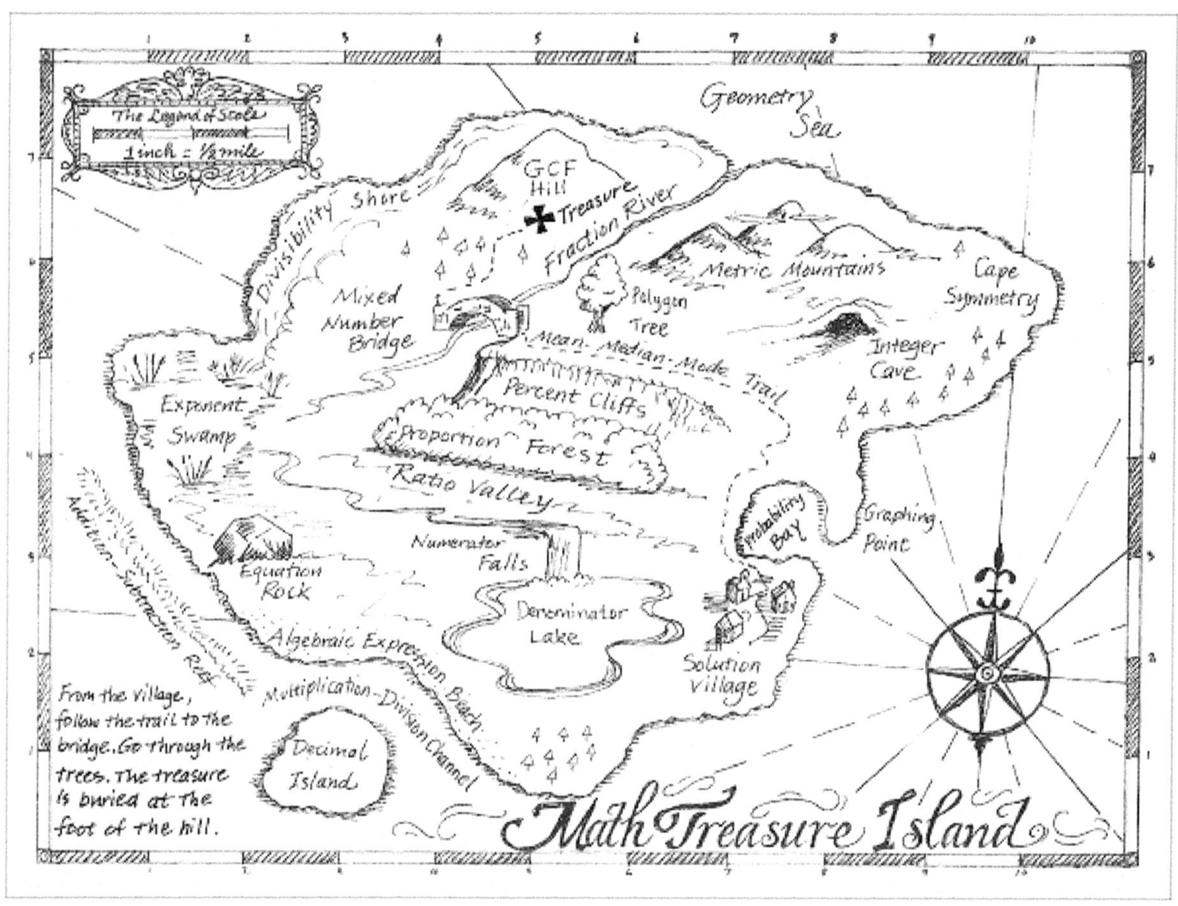

The Jungle Adventure

Name ______________________

Project: Make a poster showing an illustrated chart of a simple food chain in a jungle habitat.

Materials: 9 x 12 poster board, pictures from magazines and/or the Internet, ruler, pen.

How to make it: Using pictures and writing show a typical jungle food web. Write a description for each "link" in the food chains.

Research: Use your science textbook and the Internet.

Follow-up: What would happen if one "link" in the chain were removed? Why is it important for us to know about food chains and food webs?

____

____

____

____

____

____

____

____

____

____

____

____

The Chef's Kitchen Adventure

Name ____________________

Project: Make pancakes and see which ones are the fluffiest.

Ingredients: 2 cups flour, 1 tablespoon sugar, 1/2 teaspoon salt, 1 egg, 1 1/2 cups milk, 3 tablespoons melted butter, baking powder.

How to make them: Mix well all the ingredients except the baking powder. Divide into 3 equal batches. Add 1 teaspoon baking powder to one batch and 2 teaspoons baking powder to another. Add no baking powder to the third batch. Mix well.

Heat a lightly oiled griddle or frying pan over medium high heat. Pour or scoop the batter onto the griddle, using approximately 1/4 cup for each pancake. Brown on both sides and serve hot.

Data: Record your observations in the space below. Which recipe made the fluffiest pancakes? If you have a scale and can weigh the pancakes, record that data. In the spaces provided make drawings of the 3 kinds of pancakes and label them. What can you conclude?

____________________ ____________________ ____________________

____

____

____

____

____

The Abandoned Mine Adventure   Name ____________________

Project: Make treasure stones or rock candy.

Materials for treasure stones: 1 cup flour, 1 cup used coffee grounds, 1/2 cup salt, 1/4 cup sand, 1 cup water

How to make them: Mix all the dry ingredients together. Slowly add the water to make a stiff dough; you might end up using only half the water. Knead on a floured surface until fairly smooth. Break the dough into desired rock sizes. Hide surprises in the center of a ball of dough. Set in a safe place until totally dry, about 3 - 4 days.

Once it is dry, the dough will look and feel like a rock. You can carefully break open the home-made rocks with a hammer to reveal the hidden treasures inside.

Materials for rock candy: 1 cup water, 3 cups sugar, spoon, food coloring, string, pencil, paper clip.

How to make it: Boil the water and pour into a glass canning jar. Stir in the sugar slowly, about a teaspoon at a time. Don't rush this step. Continue until the sugar is no longer dissolving but is starting to collect at the bottom of the jar. Choose a color for your crystals and add a couple drops of food coloring. Tie one end of a piece of string around the middle of a pencil and tie a paper clip to the other end. Place the pencil over the jar so that the string hangs down and the paper clip almost touches the bottom of the jar. Allow jar to sit someplace where it will be undisturbed. Check after about 24 hours. Leave undisturbed for 3-4 days.

Safety: Use caution around the hot water.

Follow-up: Write your observations in the space below.

____

____

____

____

____

____

____

The High Mountain Adventure Name ______________________

Project: Make a board game.

Materials: Poster board, 3 x 5 cards, colored markers, pen.

How to make it: On the poster board, draw a mountain with a path that goes from the bottom to the top. Divide the path into steps. Write math problems on the 3 x 5 cards with the answers on the backs of the cards. Make 1, 2, and 3 step cards with the 1-step cards being the easiest and the 3-step cards being the most difficult.

Play the game. The winner is the first person to reach the top.

Follow-up: Write your observations in the space below. What is a good number of steps so the game is fun?

____

____

____

____

____

____

____

____

____

____

____

____

Climb the Mountain Game
20
19
18
17
16
15
Super! You can do it!
14
13
12
11
10
9
8
Keep on going. You're doing great
7
6
5
4
3
2
1
Climb the mountain - start right here. You can do it - have no fear!

The Music Conservatory Adventure Name ____________________

Project: Make a musical instrument using math.

Materials: See the attached detailed instructions.

Make an instrument: Make either wind chimes, a glass xylophone, or a plumber's pipe flute. Making these instrument requires careful measuring.

Learn to play a song on your instrument. Then record your observations in the space below.

____

____

____

____

____

____

____

____

____

____

____

____

____

____

____

____

Wind chimes

Materials: 4 feet of 1/2-inch Electrical Metallic Tubing (EMT) pipe, 2 circular wooden disks—one 3" in diameter and another 1" in diameter, monofilament fishing line, drill, screw eyes, metal or plastic ring for hanging.

How to make it: Using a pipe cutter (not a saw), cut 4 pieces of EMT: 30.4 cm, 28.6 cm, 26.8 cm, and 24.6 cm in length. Drill 8 holes in the larger disk. Drill 2 holes in each pipe on opposite sides about 1 1/2 inch from one end (as shown in the illustration).

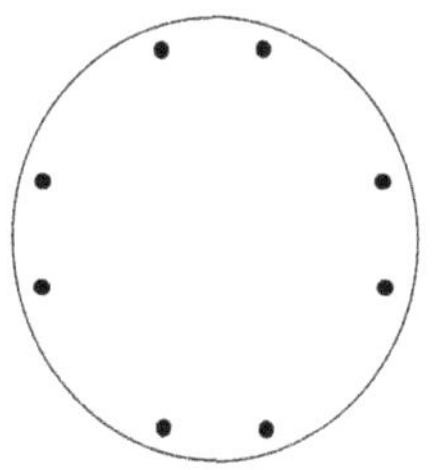

3 inch wood disk with 8 holes drilled in it.

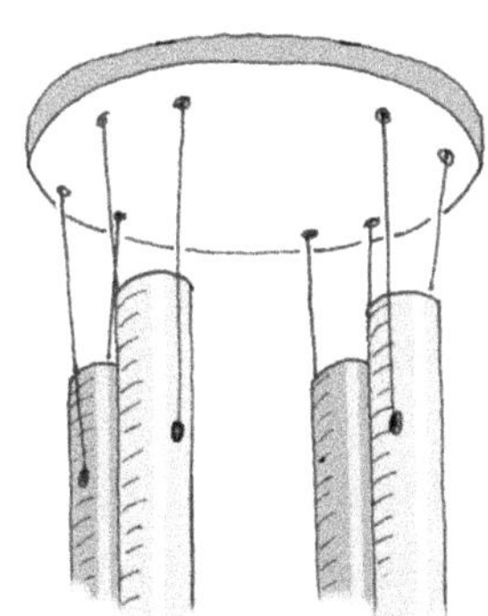

Lace the fishing line through the holes in the disk and the pipes so they look like this. The tops of the tubes should all be even.

1-inch wood disk positioned so that it will strike the metal tubes in their centers. A triangle made of plastic or wood hangs below. It catches the wind.

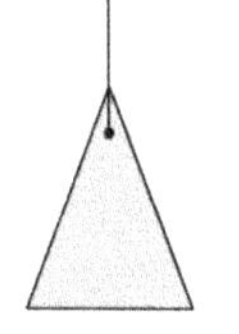

Glass Xylophone

Materials: Five to eight 20-ounce glass juice bottles or similar glass containers, water, eyedropper, metal spoon.

How to make it: Put different amounts of water in the bottles. Leave one empty. Adjust the water levels (you can use the eyedropper for fine "tuning") so it sounds like a musical scale when you strike the bottles on their sides with the spoon. Measure the columns of air in each bottle.

Safety: Be careful when handling objects made of glass.

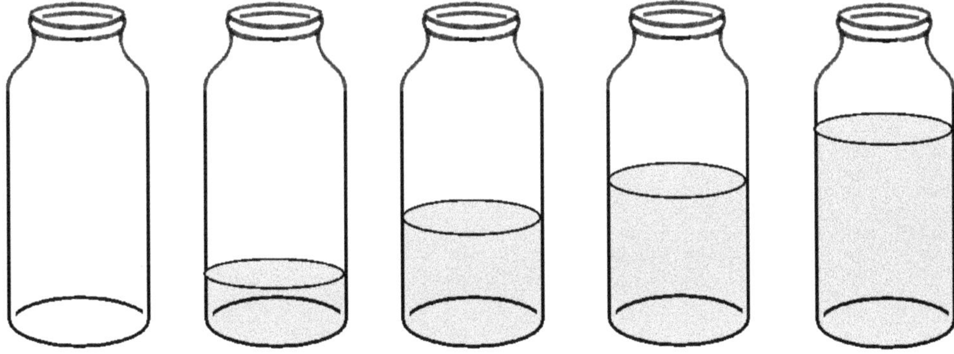

B

A

B

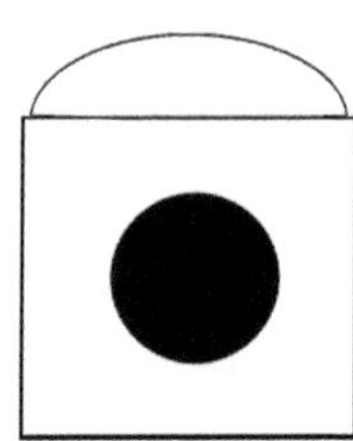

Plumber's Pipe Flute

Materials: A length of 3/4 inch CPVC pipe that measures 15-9/16 inches plus a standard end cap.

How to make it: The pattern shows the size of each hole and its correct position on the flute tube, measured with the flute cap off. Two holes are slightly offset as shown, for easier fingering.

Cut out the pattern. Attach flap B underneath the long piece so the two sections of the pattern are joined together at B to make one piece. The end cap slides over the end marked A.

Glue on the end cap by applying glue only to the pipe. Do not put glue in the cap. Drill the hole in the end cap after it has been attached and the glue has set. The hole in the end cap should be in line with the 4 holes down the center of the pipe.

This flute was designed by Mark Shepard. For additional information, including tips for playing, visit his website at *www.markshep.com/flute.*

There is no copyright or patent on this design.

The pattern

The Number Factory Adventure Name ______________________

Project: Make a multiplication calculating wheel.

Materials: two 9-inch paper plates, scissors, pen, and paper fastener.

How to make it: 1. Cut out the pattern around the outside of circle A and trace it onto a paper plate. Mark the center and cut out the circle out of the plate. 3. Cut out the smaller circle (B) in the pattern and glue it to another paper plate. Cut it out. Cut out the windows (8 small rectangles that the arrows point to). 4. Put the two plates together with a fastener through the center. 5. Fill in the numbers along the rim and the answers which go in the windows.

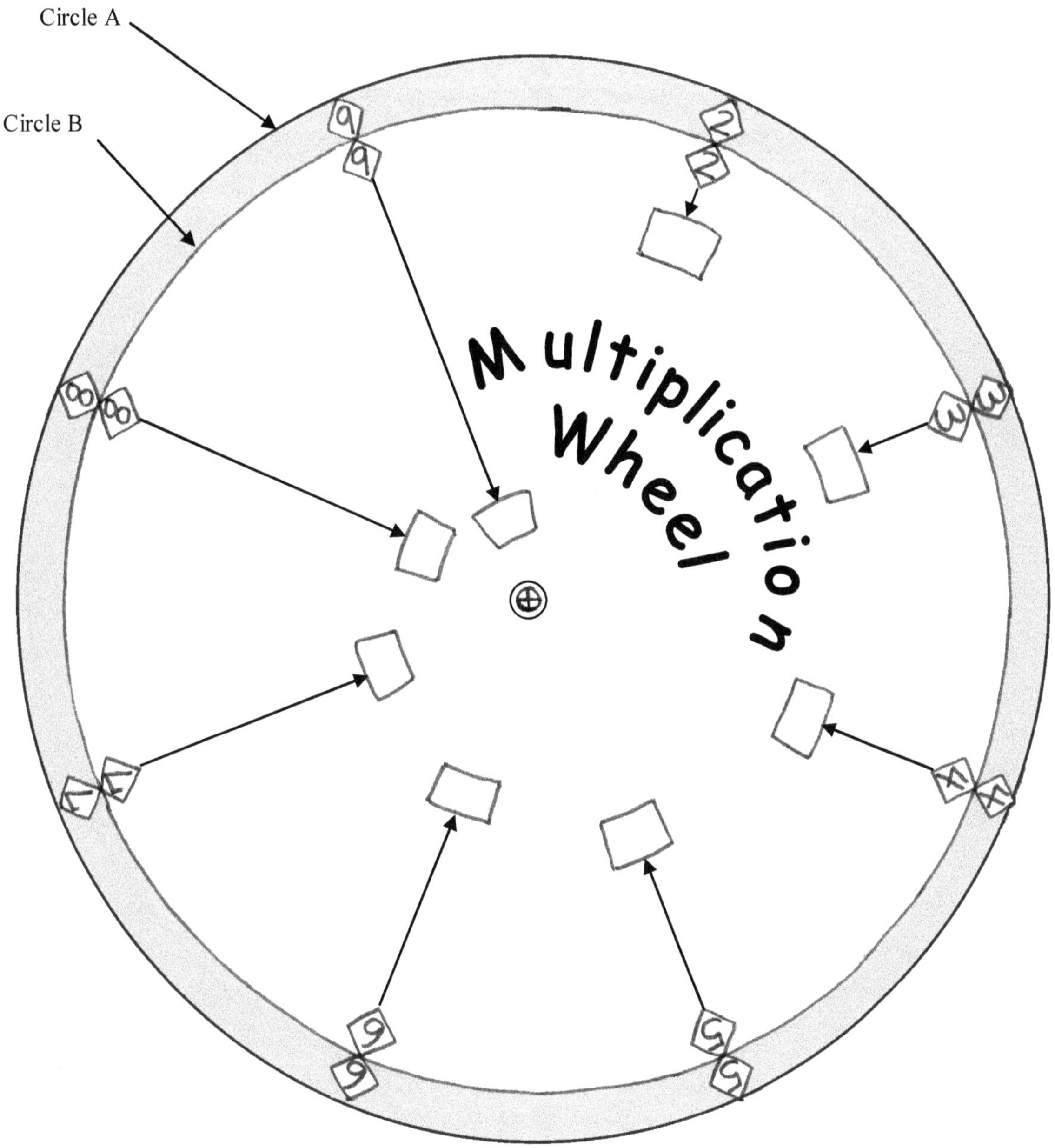

Circle A

Circle B

Multiplication Wheel

The Observatory Adventure Name ______________________

Project: Make a starfinder sky map.

Materials: two 9-inch paper plates or poster paper, a paper fastener.

How to put it together: Cut out the outside circle (the one with the names of the months) and the inside circle. Glue each of them to a separate paper plate or poster paper. Trim away the extra paper plate around the inside circle and center it on the plate with the outside circle. Punch a hole through the center (Polaris) and insert a paper fastener. Make sure the inside disk turns easily.

To Use: Keep the big arrow pointing up. Turn the inside disk until the time lines up with the date

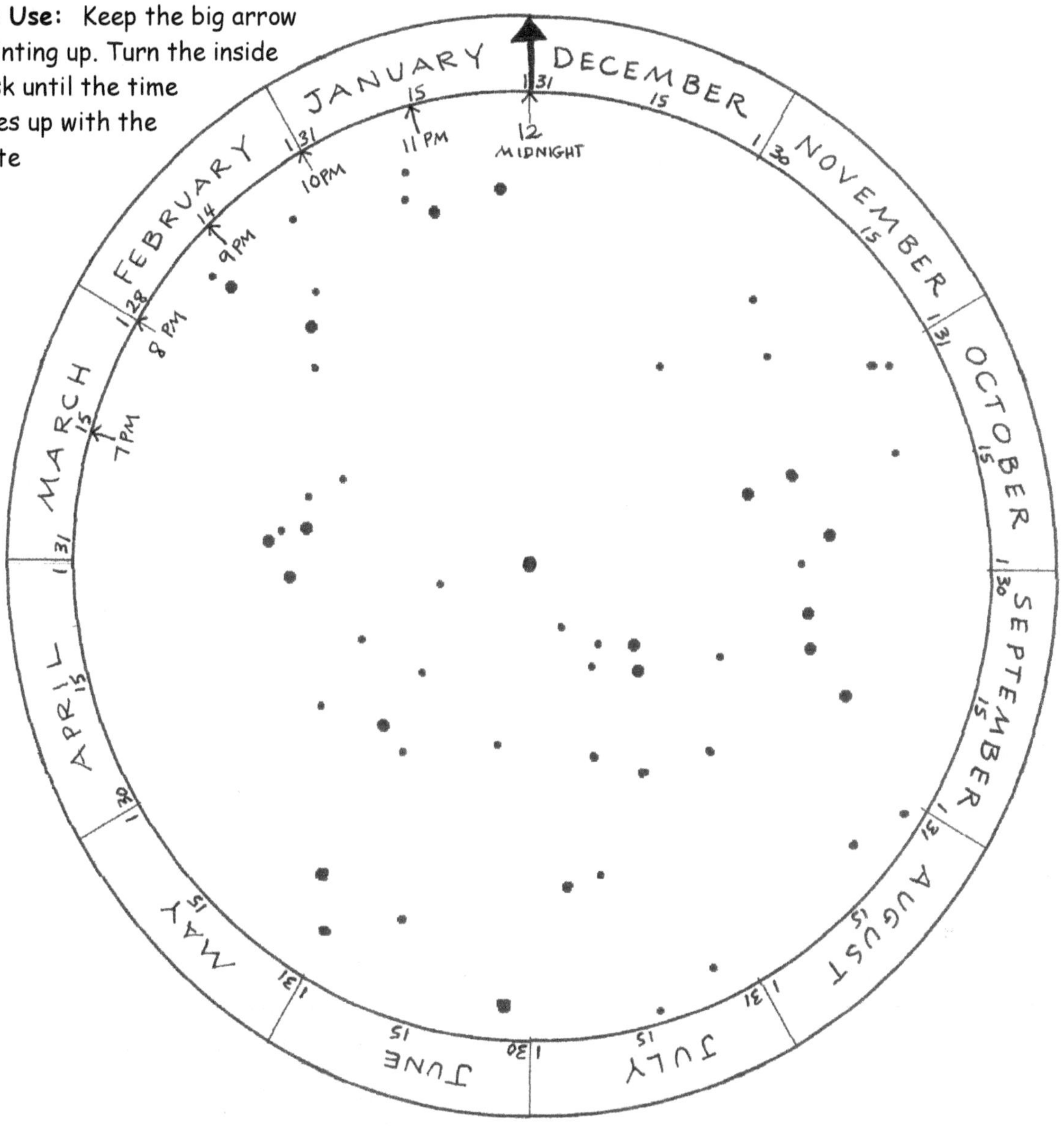

JANUARY 15 31
DECEMBER 1 15 31
NOVEMBER 1 15 30
OCTOBER 1 15 31
SEPTEMBER 1 15 30
AUGUST 1 15 31
JULY 1 15 31
JUNE 1 15 30
MAY 1 15 31
APRIL 1 15 30
MARCH 1 15 31
FEBRUARY 1 14 28

12 MIDNIGHT
11 PM
10PM
9PM
8 PM
7PM

The Race Car Adventure Name ____________________

Project: Make a rubber band race car.

Materials: cardboard, metal axles, soda straw, wheels (can be made from cardboard), craft sticks, tape, glue, rubber bands.

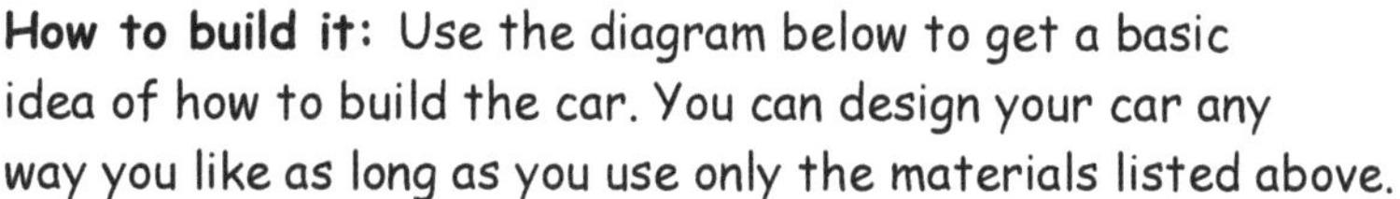

How to build it: Use the diagram below to get a basic idea of how to build the car. You can design your car any way you like as long as you use only the materials listed above.

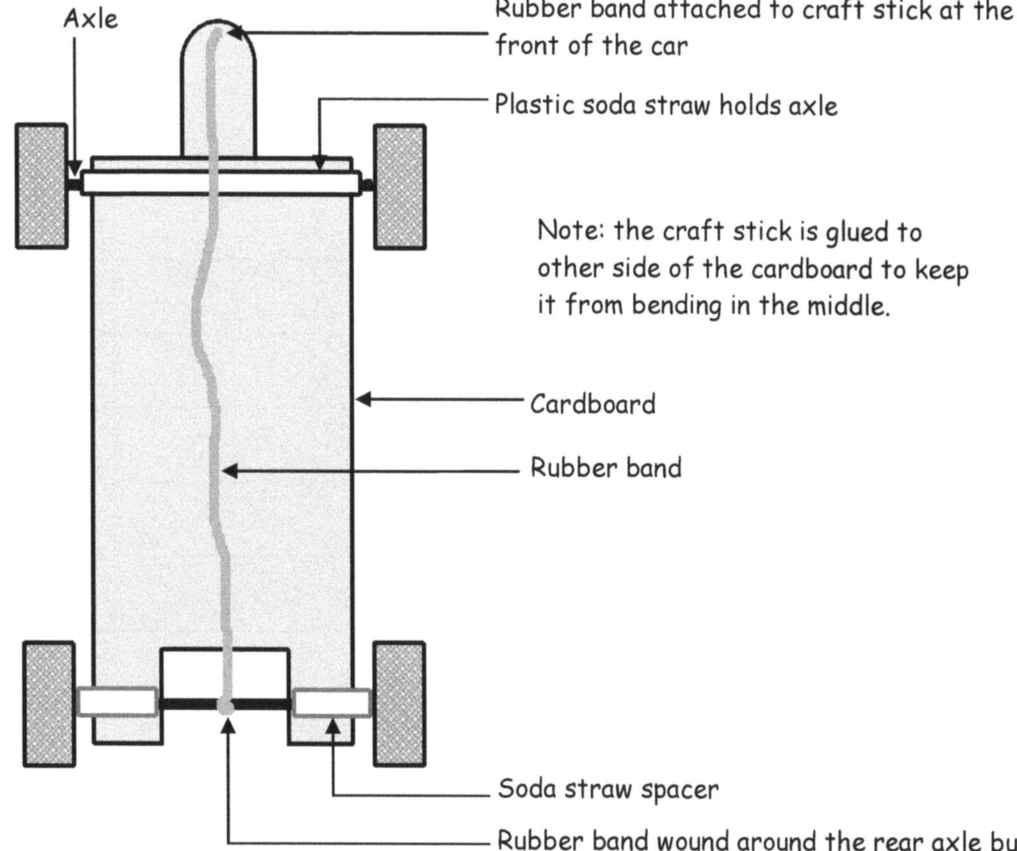

The old conductor says, "The longer the rubber band is and the larger the wheels are, the farther your car will be able to travel."

How far did your car travel? ______________

The Robot Workshop Adventure   Name ______________________

Project: Make a working animatronic (robot) hand.

Instructions: There are two websites that have instructions for making robot hands. Look at the websites and follow the instructions given on one of the sites.

One of the websites is at
www.yesmag.bc.ca/projects/robo_hand.html
This website explains how to make a simple robot hand with cardboard, straws, rubber bands, and strings.

The second website explains how to make a more sophisticated and sturdier robot hand with supplies you can find at most hardware stores. The URL is
www.instructables.com/id/Simple-Animatronics-robotic-hand/

Experiment with the robot hand to see what you can do with it. Describe what you did.

____

____

____

____

____

____

____

____

____

____

____

____

____

The Rocket Adventure

Name ______________________

Project: Make a paper rocket.
Materials: Use a rolled piece of paper for the rocket body and paper for the fins and a nose cone.
The Rocket body: Roll a piece of paper into a cylinder that has a diameter of approximately 1/2 inch. Use glue to secure it.
How To Launch: You may experiment using a straw as the launcher or launching by hand. To use a straw, insert the smaller straw into the rocket and blow. Note: air pressure launchers are available on the Internet. These will launch a paper rocket hundreds of feet in the air.

See how high and how far you can make your rocket go. Build and use a an altitude gauge to measure your rocket's altitude.

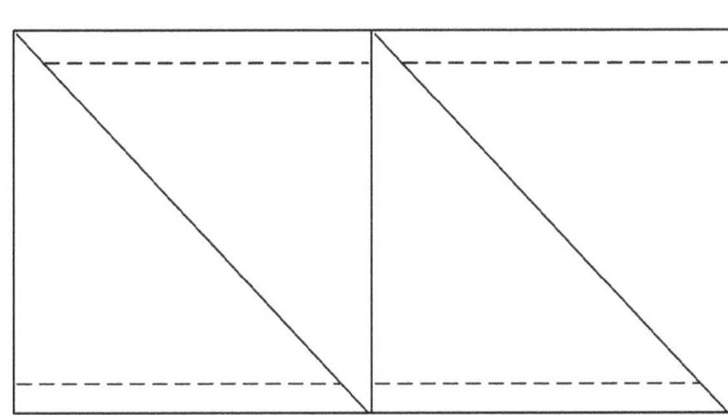

Sample fins: You can use this design to create 4 fins.

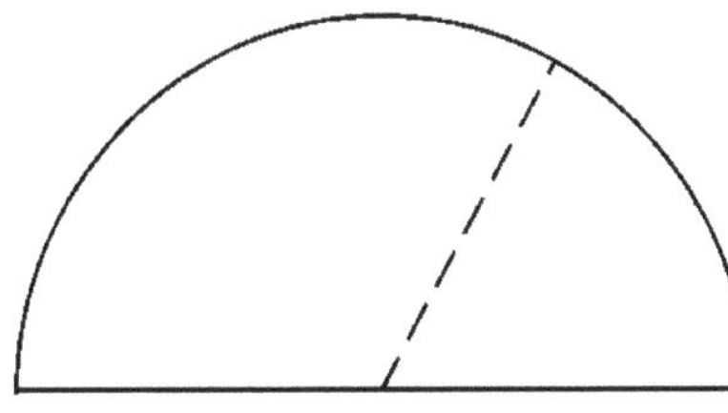

Sample nose cone: You can use this design to create a nose cone. The dotted line shows how far to overlap it.

Have a contest to see who can hit a target from the greatest distance.

The Speed Boat Adventure

Name ______________________

Project: Make a boat and measure how much weight it will hold and still float. Calculate the buoyancy.
Materials: 1 piece of 8.5 x 11 inch card stock paper, 30x45 cm of aluminum foil, 75cm duct tape, and 4 soda straws.
What to Do: Take boat design notes which include scale drawings, a list of materials, and the approximate volume. Place your boat in the test tank. Slowly add pennies until your boat sinks. Calculate the weight your boat will hold before it sinks.

Test in a large sink, bucket or tank of water.

____

____

____

____

____

____

____

____

____

____

The Time Machine Adventure   Name ___________________________

Project: Make a catapult.

Materials: clothes pin, popsicle stick, an 8-10 inch strip of 1 x 2 wood, hand saw, a bottle cap, and some hot glue or regular white glue.

How to make it: Saw a small piece off the end of the wood strip. Glue the parts together as shown in the illustration.

How to use it: Place a small Styrofoam ball in the cup, pull down and fire!

Data: See how many times you can get the ball to land in a target (plastic bucket) at various distances. Make a table below which shows the percent of accuracy.

Additional research: What kinds of catapults were used in ancient warfare? Are any catapults used today?

The Tall Tower Adventure Name ______________________

Project: Make a tower out of spaghetti and gum drops.

Materials: 50 pieces of uncooked spaghetti, 1 cup of miniature marshmallows, 10 gum drops.

How to build it: Use the marshmallows and gum drops to join the pieces of spaghetti together. Your tower must be able to stand by itself without being supported by another object or against the wall.

Data: How tall was your tower? ________________
What did you learn about how to make a structure strong?

____

____

____

Attach a photograph of yourself standing next to your tower.

The Under The Sea Adventure

Name ____________________

Project: Make a periscope

Materials: You may choose a number of different materials, 2 small mirrors, glue, tape.

How to build it: Use a paper towel roll or a couple paper milk cartons or the pattern on the next page.

Cut holes at the top and at the bottom. The two holes (or windows) should be on opposite sides. Place 2 mirrors inside tilted so you can see as shown in the diagram below.

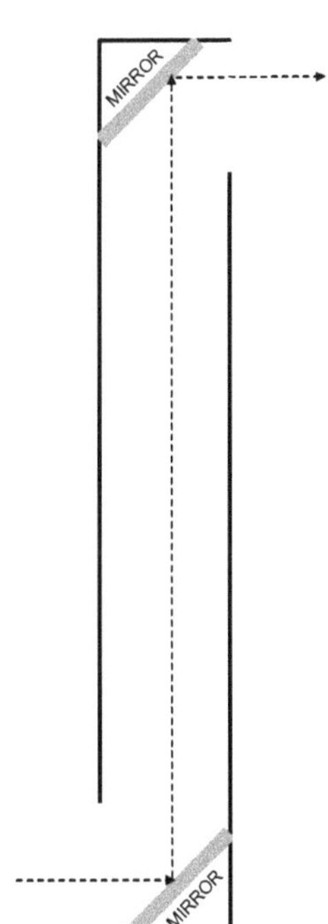

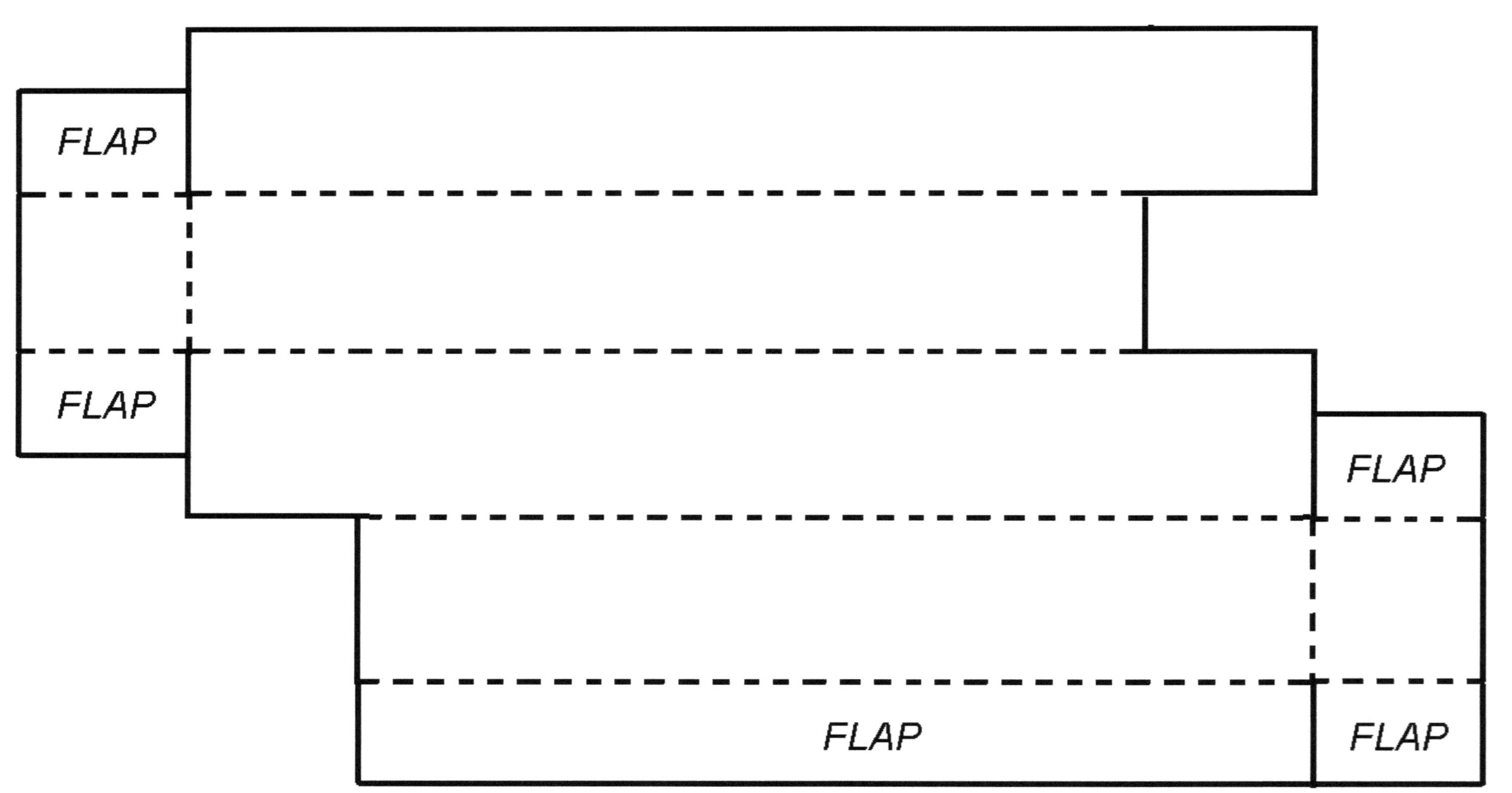
FLAP
FLAP
FLAP
FLAP
FLAP

The Video Game Adventure Name ______________________

Project: Draw a video game character.

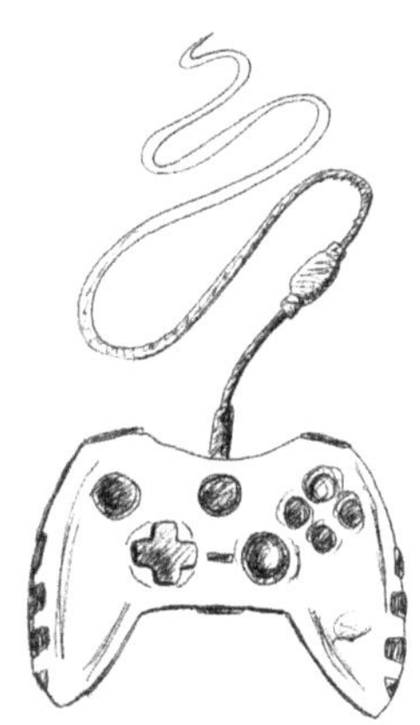

How to do it: Draw your character by coloring squares (pixels) in the graph below. Then list all of the filled in pixels. List on a separate sheet each pixel in the following way: horizontal coordinate, vertical coordinate, color. For example if you want a pixel in the lower right to be red, you would write (32, 9, red). This is the way that all video game characters are programmed.

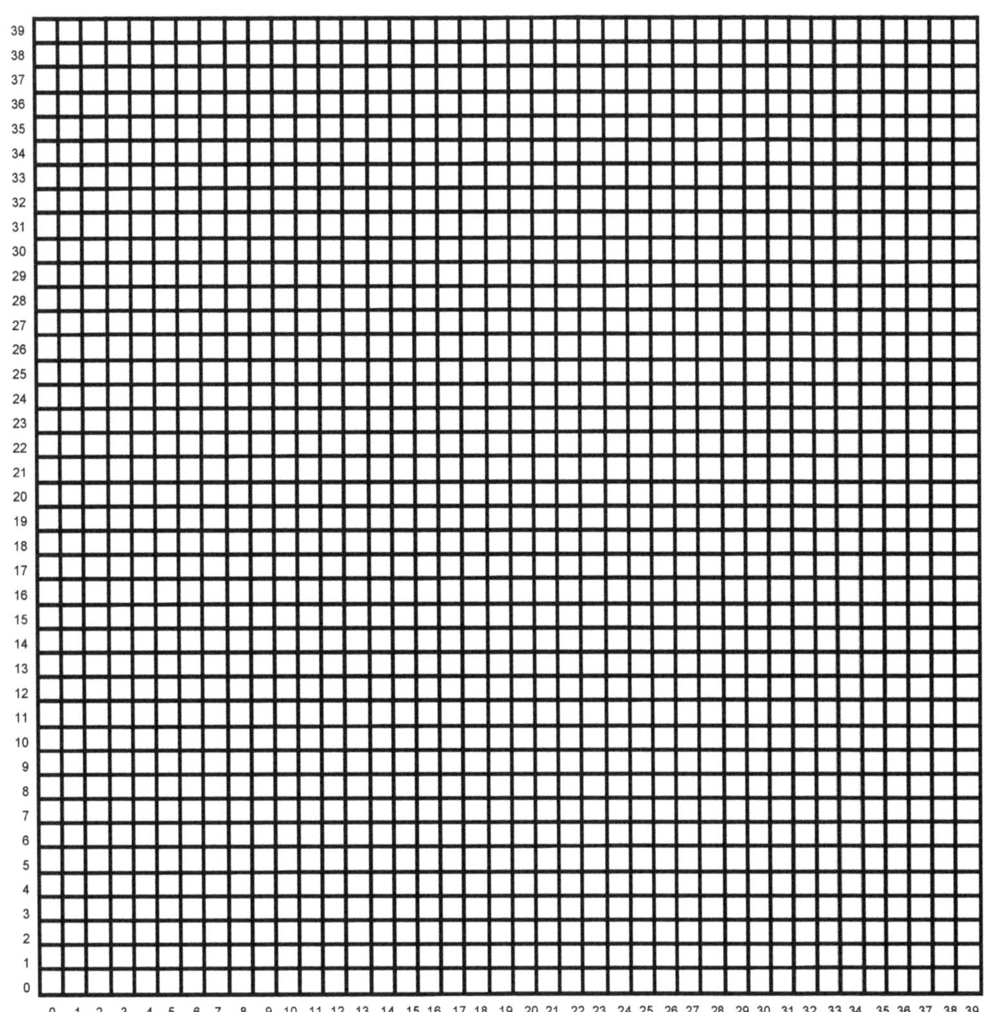

The Volcano Adventure Name ______________________

Project: Make a working model volcano

Materials: Empty 20 oz. plastic soda bottle, disposable baking pan, something to form the sides of the volcano (aluminum foil, clay, papier mache, dough made of flour, salt, and water), vinegar, baking soda, red food coloring.

How to build it: Build it in the baking pan to avoid a huge mess when the volcano erupts. First, glue the soda bottle in the center of the pan. Now sculpt the sides. Be careful not to get anything down inside the bottle.

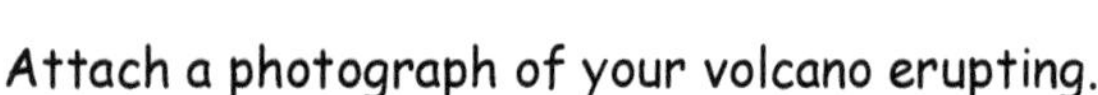

Attach a photograph of your volcano erupting.

The Eskimo Adventure   Name ________________________

Project: Build an igloo.

Materials: For blocks, use sugar cubes for a small igloo or empty paper milk cartons for a large igloo that you can actually get inside.

How to Build It: You will be building a dome with the blocks (sugar cubes or milk cartons). Begin with a circle as the base and build up from there with each layer leaning inward slightly. The blocks will have to be glued together.

How wide and tall is your igloo? _________

How many blocks did it take to build it? _________

Take a photograph of your igloo and attach it below.

The Sailing Ship Adventure

Name ________________________

Project: Build a model sailing ship.

Materials: Use any materials that you want.

What It Must Do: Your sailing ship must have a rounded hull—no flat bottom rafts. It must float and not tip over. It must have at least one sail. When you blow on the sail, your ship must go forward in a straight line through the water.

Record how you built your ship, listing the materials and the dimensions. Also, record how you solved the problem of getting the ship to float upright without tipping over and how you designed it so it would sail in a straight line.

____

____

____

____

____

____

____

____

____

____

____

____

____

____

Make a game board. Cut out the following 12 images and tape them together or mount them on a poster board.

DRAW A
CHANCE
CARD
ADVENTU

DRAW A
CHANCE
CARD
DRAW A
CHANCE
CARD
URE EXPRE

ADVENTURE SITE
SELECT AN ADVENTURE CARD
ESS
DRAW A CHANCE CARD

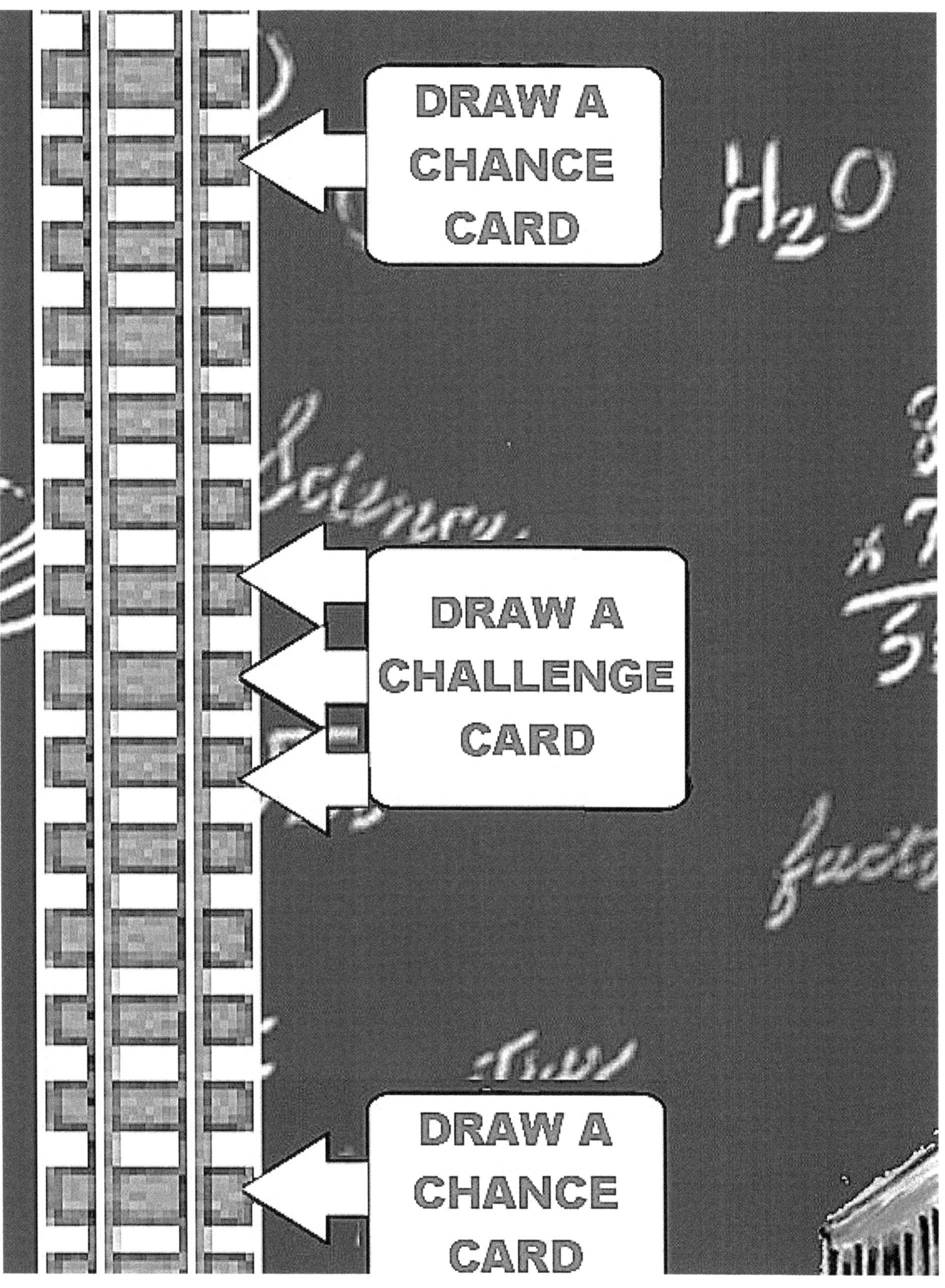
DRAW A CHANCE CARD
H_2O
DRAW A CHALLENGE CARD
DRAW A CHANCE CARD

Math
ADVENTURE EXPRESS

Math
8
x 7
56
factors

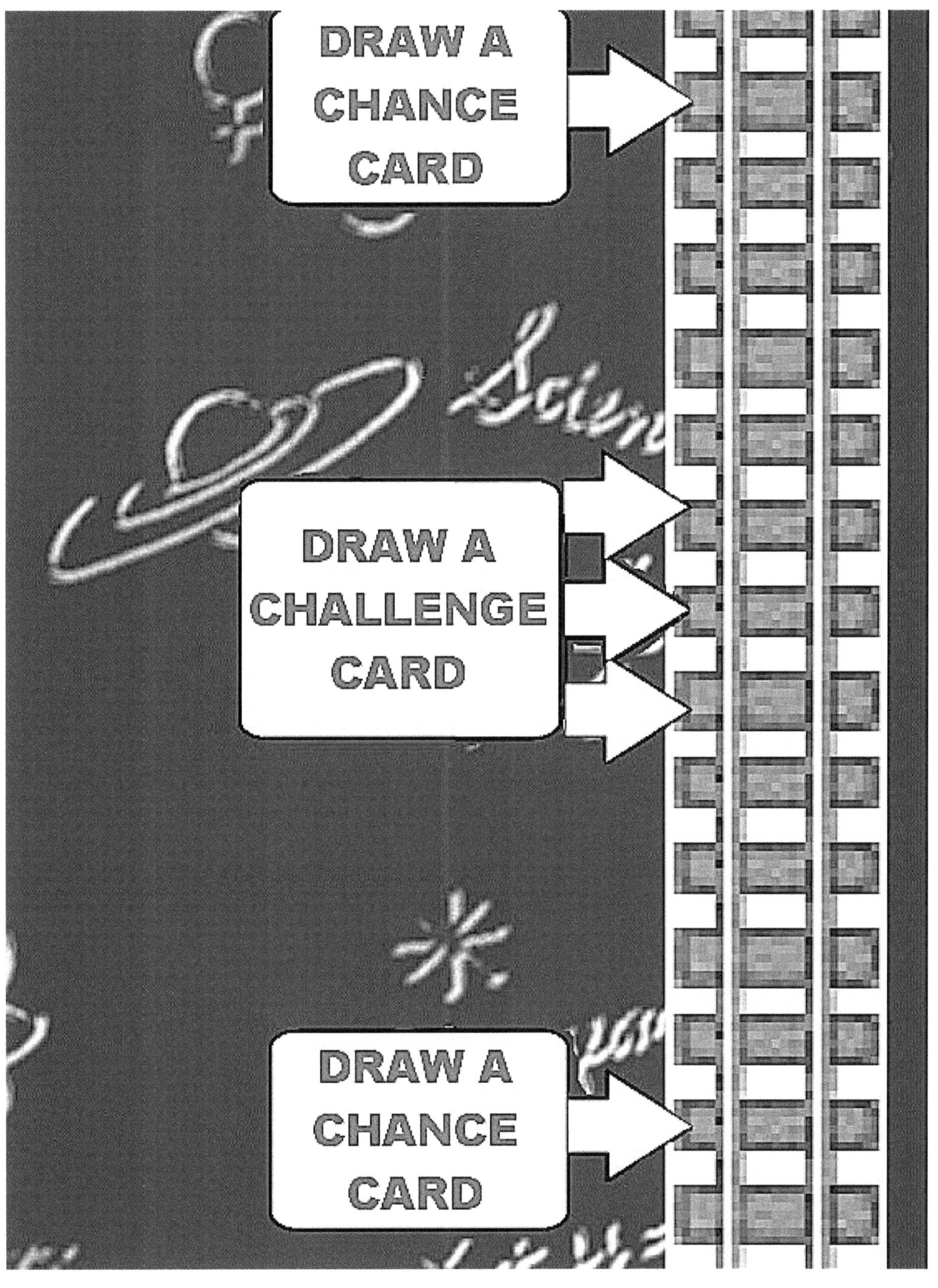
DRAW A
CHANCE
CARD
DRAW A
CHALLENGE
CARD
DRAW A
CHANCE
CARD

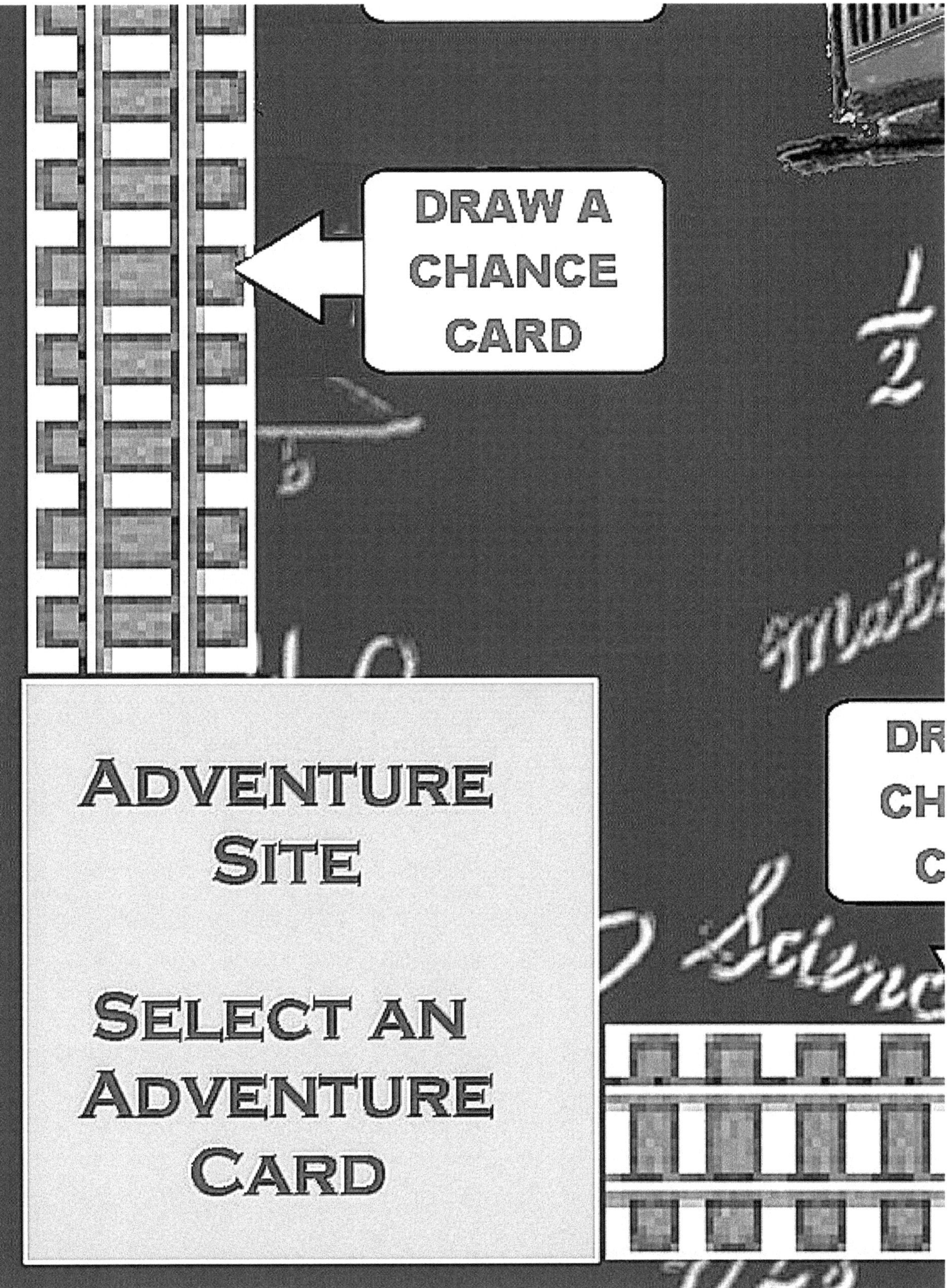
DRAW A
CHANCE
CARD
Math
Science
ADVENTURE
SITE
SELECT AN
ADVENTURE
CARD

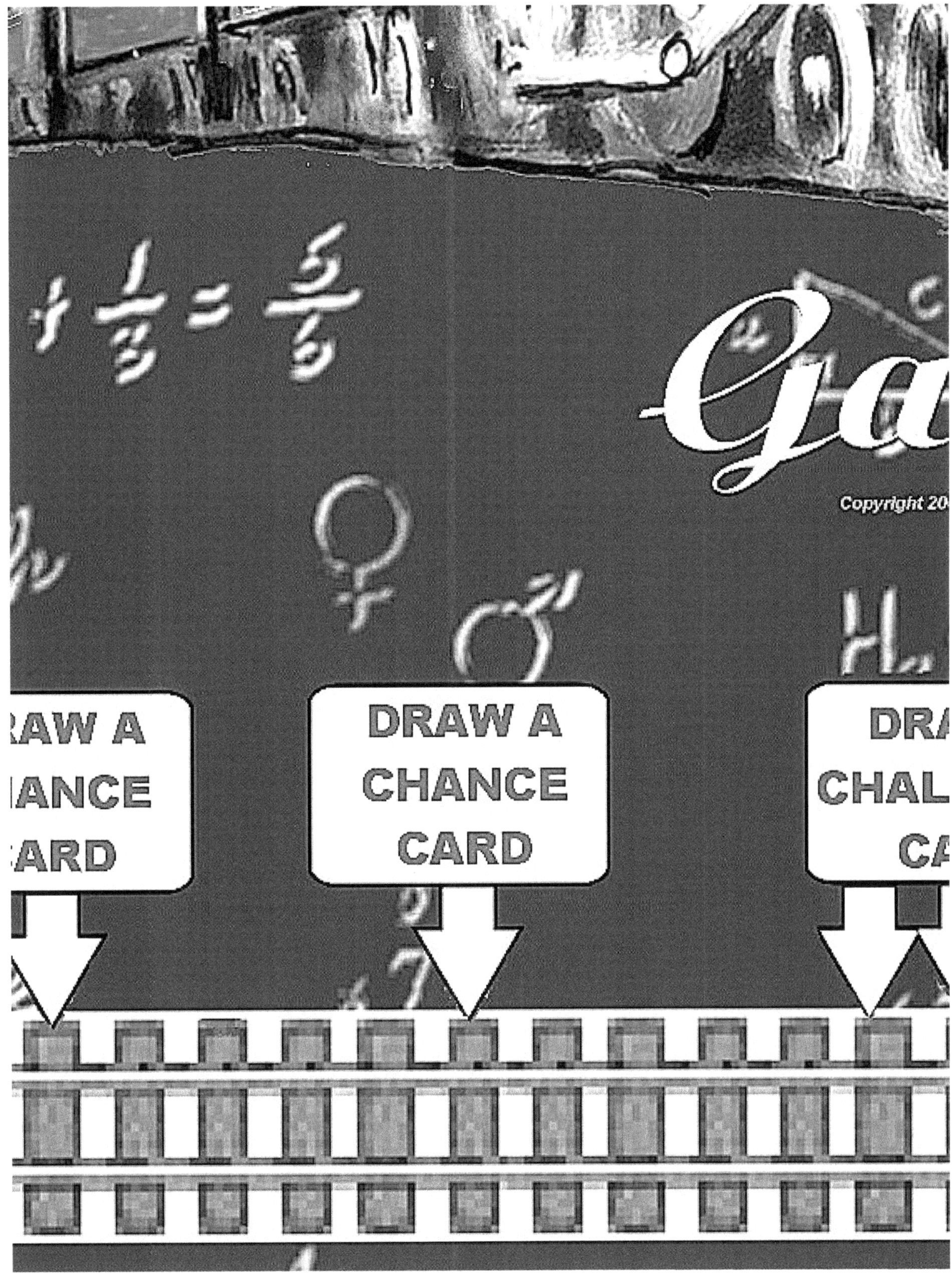

RAW A
ANCE
ARD
DRAW A
CHANCE
CARD
DRA
CHAL
CA
Copyright 20

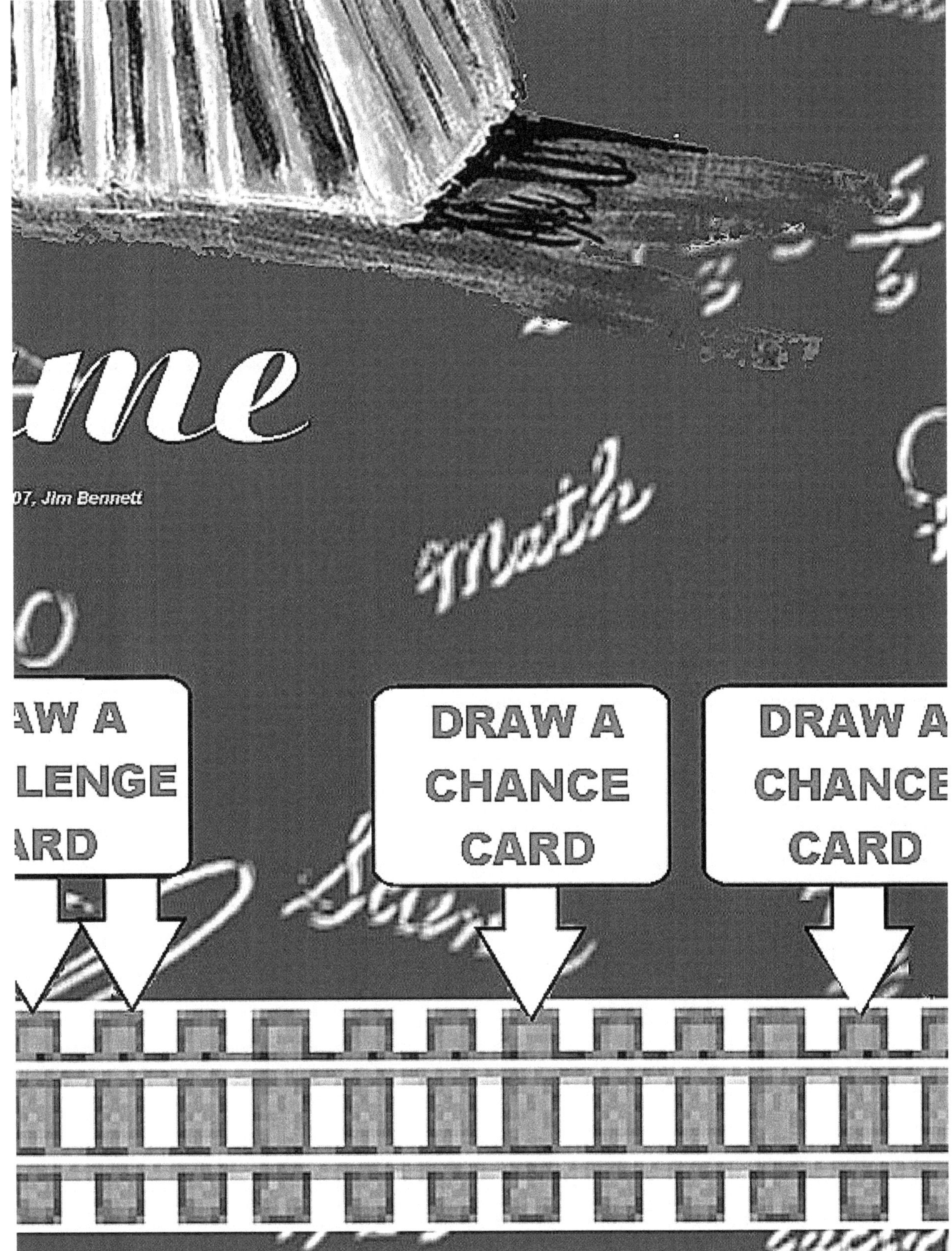
me
07, Jim Bennett
Math
AW A
LENGE
ARD
DRAW A
CHANCE
CARD
DRAW A
CHANCE
CARD

DRAW A
CHANCE
CARD

H_2O

TRAIN STATION

NOTES

NOTES

NOTES

www.ingramcontent.com/pod-product-compliance
Ingram Content Group UK Ltd.
Pitfield, Milton Keynes, MK11 3LW, UK
UKHW051137260726
13967UKWH00010B/3099

9 781435 750524